In the same series:

The Louvre
Musée d'Orsay
The Impressionists
Picasso
Paris

Front cover :
"Icarus", plate VIII of *Jazz*, 1943

Passage L'homme – 26 rue de Charonne – 75011 Paris

ISBN 2-86656-199-6

KEY ART WORKS

Matisse

at the Musée National d'Art Moderne
MNAM-CCI
Centre Georges Pompidou

Anette Robinson
in collaboration with Isabelle Bréda
Translated by Trista Selous

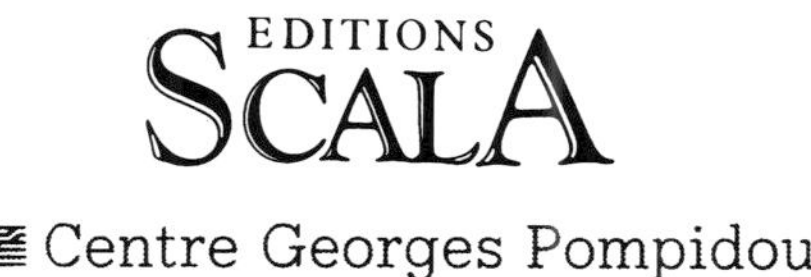

Centre Georges Pompidou

Acknowledgements

We should like to thank the following for assistance with picture research:
Christian Arthaud (Musée Matisse, Nice), Jeanne Sudour (Musée Picasso, Paris)
Isabelle Varloteaux (Musée des Beaux-Arts, Grenoble)
Laurent Giovannoni (Musée Matisse, Le Cateau-Cambrésis)
Missody Zrihen, Florence Villiers-Perrard and Brigitte Vincent (MNAM, Paris).
We should also particularly like to thank
Terence Robinson for his constant help.

All works reproduced here are by Henri Matisse, unless a different artist's name is given. They are all part of the collection of the Musée National d'Art Moderne, unless a different source is given. In the captions the place mentioned after a picture's title indicates where it was painted.

To the reader

The underlying aim of the KEY ART WORKS series is to develop the reader's sense of how to look at a work of art, thinking about its form, colour and theme and comparing it to other works. Each book is arranged around a presentation of twelve works selected from the collections of a particular museum. These twelve then provide a starting point for the discussion of over one hundred works in all, which reveal the fundamental preoccupations of a specific artist or period in the history of art. This book presents twelve masterpieces by Matisse chosen from the collections of the Musée National d'Art Moderne, Centre Georges Pompidou.

◆ The **Introduction** describes the different places in France where Matisse's works can be seen and provides a brief history of the collections. These include museums in Paris, in Matisse's native town of Le Câteau-Cambrésis, Nice, Saint-Paul-de-Vence, Grenoble and many other places.

◆ The **twelve selected works** are analysed in detail, gradually revealing the scope of Matisse's work and some of its key elements.

◆ These analyses are arranged in **six chapters**, dealing with different aspects of the artist's work: his favourite themes (still-life, the studio, the female nude), the various domains he explored (painting, sculpture, illustrated books, collage, stained glass) and the never-ending research into purity of line and colour to which he devoted his life.

◆ Additional vital information is supplied in the **appendices**:

- An illustrated biography
- Matisse as seen by his friends in letters and quotations
- A glossary

Contents

Matisse in France – A history of the collections 10

Matisse and the silent life of things **17**
First Orange Still-life 21
Still-life on a Green Sideboard 27

Matisse, or colour unleashed **33**
Luxe, calme et volupté 37

Matisse, or a particular idea of beauty **43**
The Back I, II, III, IV 47
The Dancer 53
The Romanian Blouse 61

Matisse and the theme of the window **67**
The Painter in his Studio 71
The Violinist at the Window 77
Large Red Interior 83

Matisse: writing and the image **89**
Jazz 93

Matisse and drawing within painting **99**
Pale Blue Window 103

A step-by-step analysis **109**
The Sorrow of the King

Biography 112
Matisse seen by his friends 118
Glossary 123

Matisse in France

History of the collections

A man of the North,
drawn to the light of the South,
Matisse gave his name
to two museums:
one in his home town in the North,
the other in Nice, in the South
he could not bear to leave.
Many museums
hold some of his works,
but it is the Musée National
d'Art Moderne in the Centre
Georges Pompidou, Paris,
that has the greatest number
of masterpieces by Matisse,
who devoted more than 60 years
of his life to his art.

Matisse with his birds, ►
Nice, 1938.
Photograph by
Roger Schall.

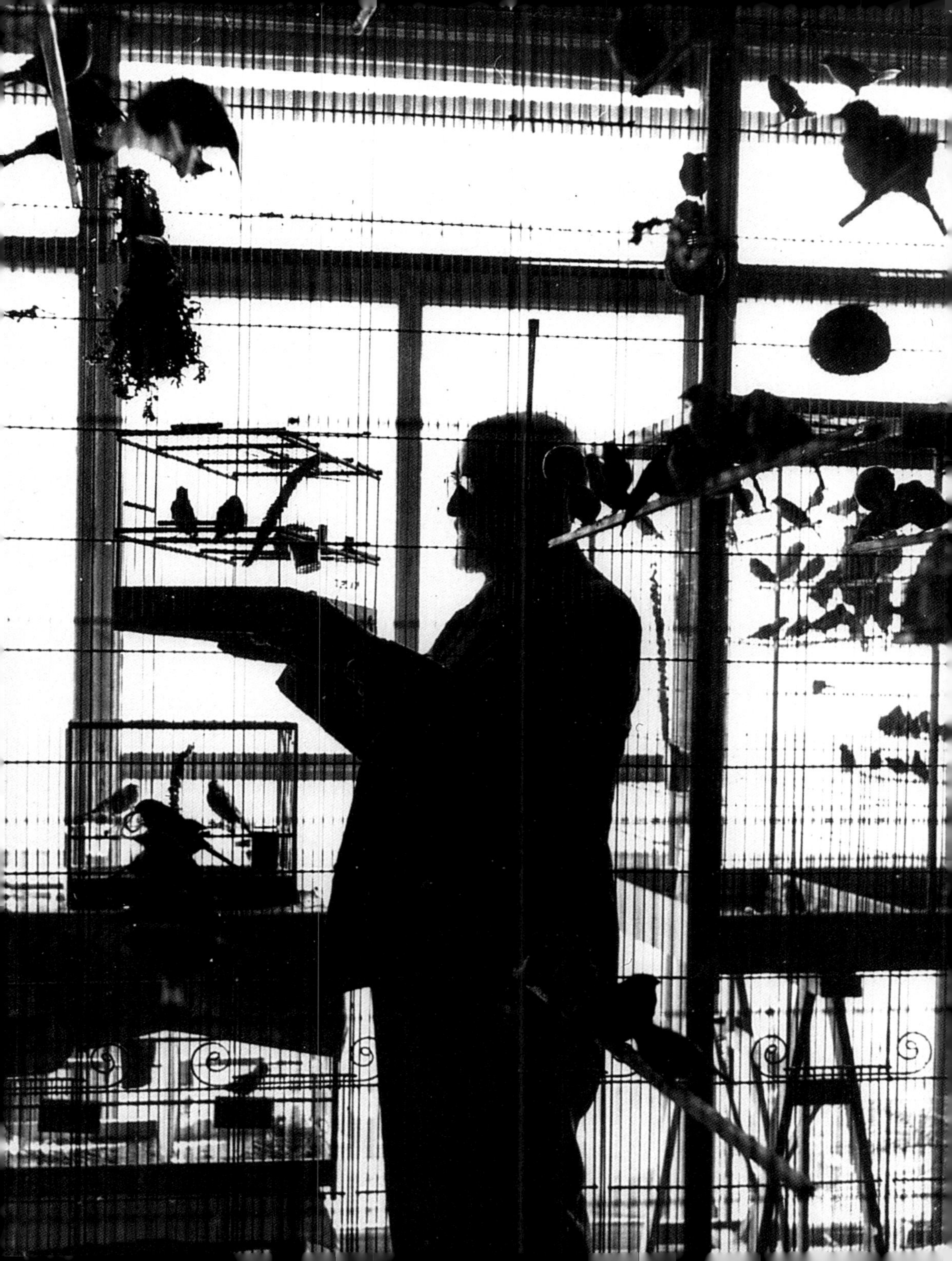

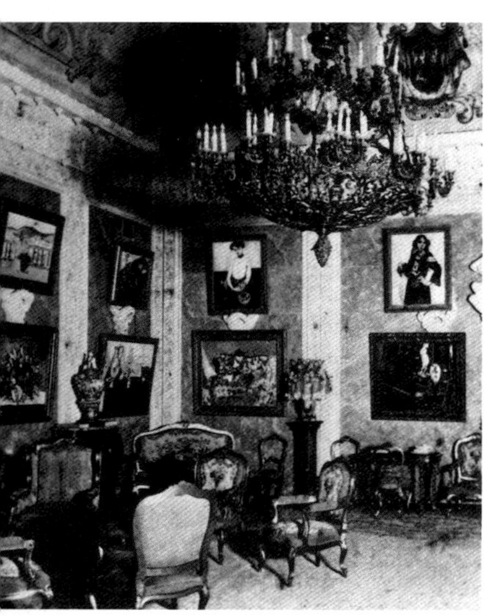

▲
Sergey Shchukin's drawing-room, Moscow, 1912.

At a time when Matisse retrospectives attract hundreds of thousands of visitors, it is hard to believe that he almost gave up painting for lack of buyers. In 1904, aged 35 and with several exhibitions to his name, he showed his paintings at Berthe Weill's gallery, Druet and Vollard. But he sold only a very few at ridiculously low prices. To live from his painting and feed his family, which included three children, he decided to found a kind of "union" with twelve friends, each of whom would give him 200 francs. In return, Matisse would give them two paintings each a year. It was a good idea, but Matisse could find only two collectors who were willing to become involved. The first people to buy a picture by Matisse were two Americans, the Steins, who paid 500 francs for *Woman in a Hat*. This painting stirred up controversy, created a scandal and represented a turning point in Matisse's career. From now on, Michael and Sarah Stein – together with Michael's brother, Leo, and sister, Gertrude – were to play an important part in the artistic life of the time. Artists, writers and art lovers all gathered at their apartments in the Rue Madame and Rue de Fleurus in Paris. It was there that Matisse met the people who were to become his friends, such as the art critic Georges Duthuit, who later also became his son-in-law. In addition, Matisse met a number of future collectors at the Steins', especially foreigners. This explains why many of his paintings were taken out of France so soon after being painted.
Among the collectors who visited the Steins', Matisse met two American sisters from Baltimore, Claribel and Etta Cone. In 1949, on Etta's death, 43 paintings by Matisse, 18 bronze sculptures and 100 engravings were left to the Museum of Art, Baltimore. This legacy constitutes one of the most important collections of

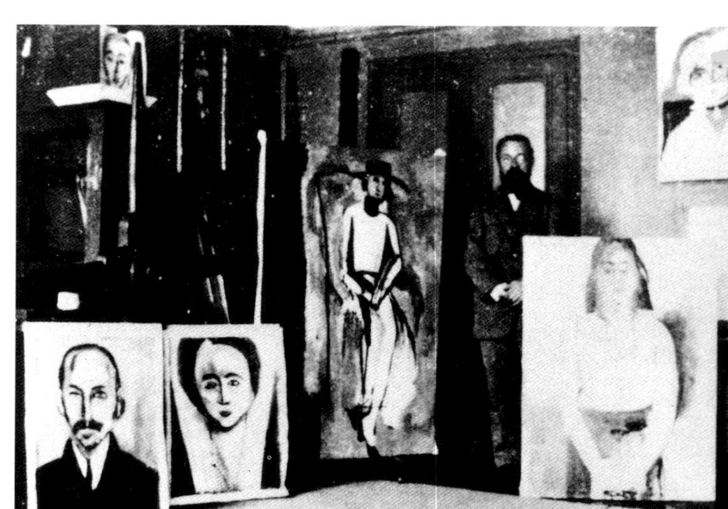

Matisse's work held outside France.

In 1917, again at Rue Madame, Matisse met Dr Barnes, an extremely rich American whose pharmaceutical business had developed a new antiseptic. Barnes was passionate about modern art. He later bought Leo Stein's entire collection, as well as those of other American collectors who were ruined in the Wall Street crash. In 1922 Barnes decided to establish a foundation at Merion, near Philadelphia, Pennsylvania, for the training of future artists. When Matisse visited him in 1930, he discovered about 100 works by Cezanne, nearly 200 by Renoir and others including some by Picasso and Soutine.

Apart from *The Dance*, a painting specially commissioned from Matisse to hang in the main hall at Merion, the Barnes Foundation owns more than 80 Matisses, including *The Joy of Living* (1905). Today its collection contains more than one thousand paintings, including early and modern works. Unfortunately they are not easily accessible. The press continually used to call him mad and describe him as being *nouveau riche*, and Barnes became angry and forbade almost all public access to his foundation. Only a few hundred visitors are allowed in each month.

◄ Matisse's studio at 19 Quai Saint-Michel, Paris, in 1916. In the studio are portraits of Michael and Sarah Stein.

It was not only the Americans who took an interest in Matisse. Shchukin, the famous Russian merchant-collector, whom the painter had met at the Steins', became one of his most important patrons. Shchukin loved the colourful works of Fauvism and commissioned for his palace in Moscow two paintings from Matisse, *Dance* and *Music* (1908). His friend Morosov, another Russian merchant-collector, was also very enthusiastic about Matisse's work. In 1918, during the Revolution, 55 paintings were seized by the state. These were shared out between the National Museum of Fine Art in Moscow (later the Pushkin Museum) and the Hermitage Museum in St Petersburg.

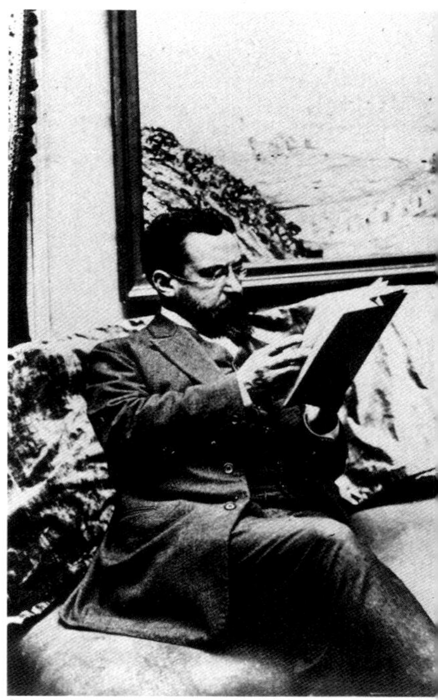

▲
Marcel Sembat, Socialist member of parliament for Montmartre.

Fortunately, many of Matisse's paintings had remained in France, thanks to such collectors as Auguste Bréal, Auguste Pellerin, Gustave Payet and, in particular, Marcel Sembat. Sembat and his wife, Georgette Agutte, were among Matisse's most ardent admirers. A year after Sembat's death in 1922, five major paintings from his collection were left to the Musée de Grenoble. Matisse donated two other works to this museum.

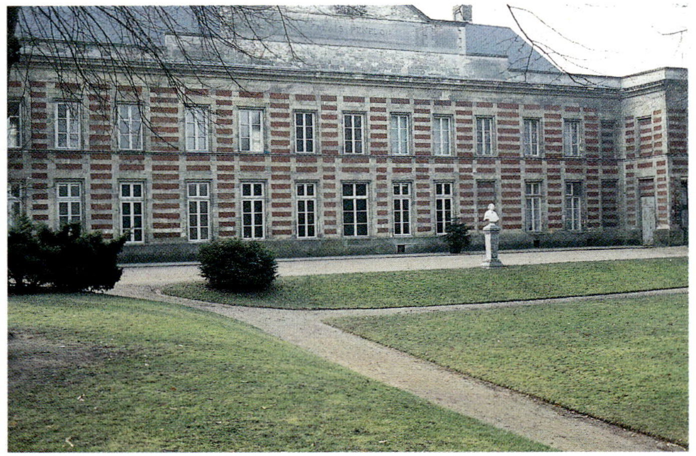

◄ The Musée Matisse in Le Cateau-Cambrésis.

Where can Matisse's work be seen in France?

Today the **Musée de Grenoble** has one of the most important collections in the country, with eight paintings, twenty-nine drawings, two ceramics, three sculptures, two etchings and one woodcut, to which three works from the Pierre Matisse *"dation"* were added in 1992.
Since 1968 heirs in France have been able to offset donations of works of art against their inheritance tax. This is known as a *"dation"*. As a result, when Matisse's younger son, Pierre, died in 1989, three paintings, thirteen sculptures and eight drawings by his father went into public collections.

The **Musée Matisse in Nice** is situated on the Colline de Cimiez in the Villa des Arènes and houses the largest collection of Matisse's work in France, outside the collections of the Musée National d'Art Moderne.
By donating two works of major importance in October 1953, *Still-life with Pomegranates* (1947) and *Creole Dancer* (1950), Henri Matisse himself provided the core of the Nice collection, which has since been enriched by donations and *"dations"* from his heirs.
Today the permanent collection of the museum contains:
- 31 paintings, including *Interior with a Harmonium* (1900), *Storm in Nice* (1919) and *Window in Tahiti* (1935-36);
- 7 large gouache cut-outs, including *The wave* (1952) and *Blue Nude IV* (1952);
- 57 sculptures in bronze and 1 in wood;
- 236 drawings;
- 218 engravings;
- 14 books illustrated by Matisse;
- 187 objects from the painter's collection.

The Musée Matisse in Nice. ►

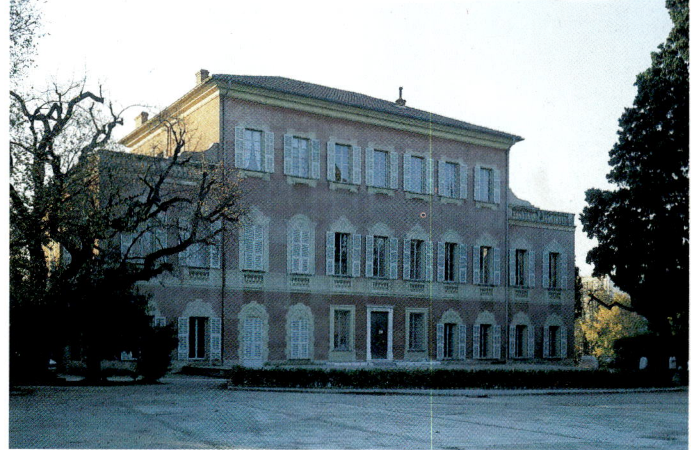

Since 1982 the **Musée Matisse in Le Cateau-Cambrésis** (Nord) has been housed in the former Fénélon Palace. It was originally founded by Matisse in 1952. The painter carefully selected which of his works he would donate to his home town. This collection has since been enriched by family donations, *"dations"* and acquisitions. Today the collection consists of:

- 16 paintings (3 in storage), including a *Self-portrait* (1918) and the penultimate picture Matisse painted: *Woman with a Blue Gandurah* (1951);
- 17 sculptures;
- 17 gouache cut-outs;
- 135 engravings;
- 70 drawings;
- 15 illustrated books.

The **Chapelle du Rosaire** in Vence was entirely designed and decorated by Matisse between 1948 and 1950 and was consecrated in June 1951. The artist's preparatory drawings and some lithographs are exhibited in a corridor adjoining the chapel.

Very close to the Chapelle du Rosaire is the **Fondation Adrien Maeght**, at Saint-Paul-de-Vence. This consists of a number of gallery rooms that have been organised like the houses of a village devoted to modern art, standing in a sculpture park. Although one room bears the name of Matisse, the Foundation itself has only one of his drawings, the *Portrait of Fabriani* (1943).

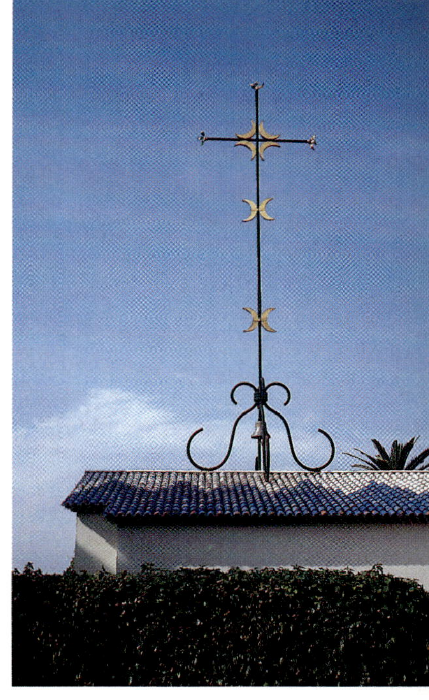

▲ The Chapelle du Rosaire in Vence.

However, many exhibitions of the painter's work have been held there.

Other museums in France contain some works by Matisse; for example, the Musée d'Art Moderne de la Ville de Paris, the Musée de l'Annonciade in Saint-Tropez, the Musée de Villeneuve d'Ascq and the museums of Dijon, Lyon, Toulouse and Besançon.

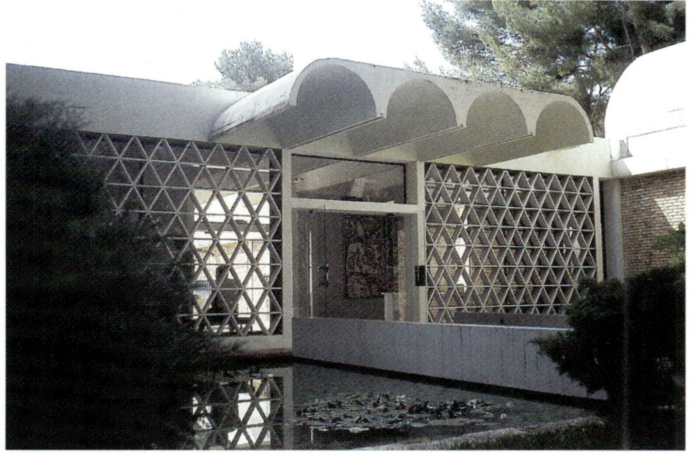

◄ The Fondation Maeght in Saint-Paul-de-Vence.

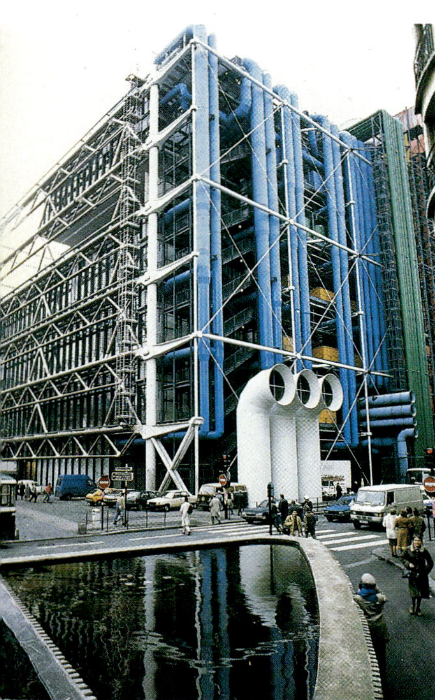

▲
External view of the Centre Georges Pompidou, Paris.
The MNAM has been housed here since 1977.

The MNAM, the Musée National d'Art Moderne, has one of the richest holdings of any museum of works by Matisse; it currently holds 271. It is as important as American, Russian and Danish museums. Today this seems perfectly natural: after all, Matisse was French, wasn't he? It is Matisse and Picasso who have left the greatest mark on the art of the 20th century. In 1944, however, the museum owned only three paintings and six drawings by Matisse. And yet that year the artist was 75 and enjoyed a world-wide reputation.

At first the state bought copies by Matisse of the old masters, works that he had painted at the end of the previous century and which were used to decorate civil servants' offices. The first time a "real" picture was bought officially was in 1922, when *Odalisque in Red Trousers* (1921) entered the Musée du Luxembourg in Paris.

When the MNAM was set up in 1945, Jean Cassou, its first curator, gathered a proper core of works by Matisse. He had a difficult task, since he had to identify which, out of all the artists working at the time, would be remembered by history.

Thanks to Cassou's far-sightedness and to his boundless admiration for Matisse, national museums began to buy the painter's works and to take an interest in what he was doing.

In 1949 the MNAM (housed in the Palais de Tokyo since 1947) exhibited Matisse's recent work for the first time ever. This comprised the complete series of Vence interiors, brush and Indian ink drawings and a great number of paper cut-outs. During the last ten years of his life, Matisse was on excellent terms with the MNAM. Well aware of its financial difficulties, he donated several of his works to the museum and sold others to it at derisory prices.

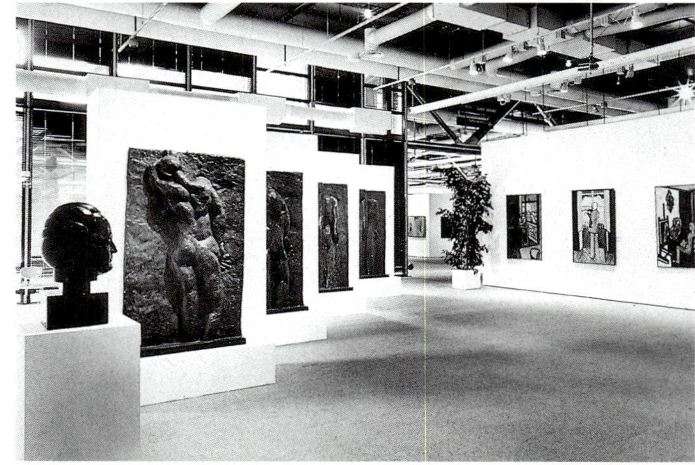

In 1965, two years after Matisse's death, the museum celebrated his work for the first time. In 1970, to mark the centenary of his birth, the Réunion des Musées Nationaux staged a major retrospective, which attracted nearly 400,000 visitors. Seven years later, when the MNAM moved to the Centre Georges Pompidou, it was finally granted its own acquisitions budget. Since then its collection of works by Matisse has been enriched by ambitious purchases, legacies, *"dations"* and donations. Today, thanks to the generosity of the artist's family, particularly the son and daughter of Jean Matisse (Henri's son), it provides an almost completely representative collection of the artistic activity and vision of Henri Matisse. All that is lacking are a few works from the Fauvist period, 1905-06, and 1910-13. The reorganisation of the MNAM galleries, overseen by the Italian architect Gae Aulenti, and the rehanging carried out in 1984, have restored Matisse's work to the position of honour that it richly deserves.

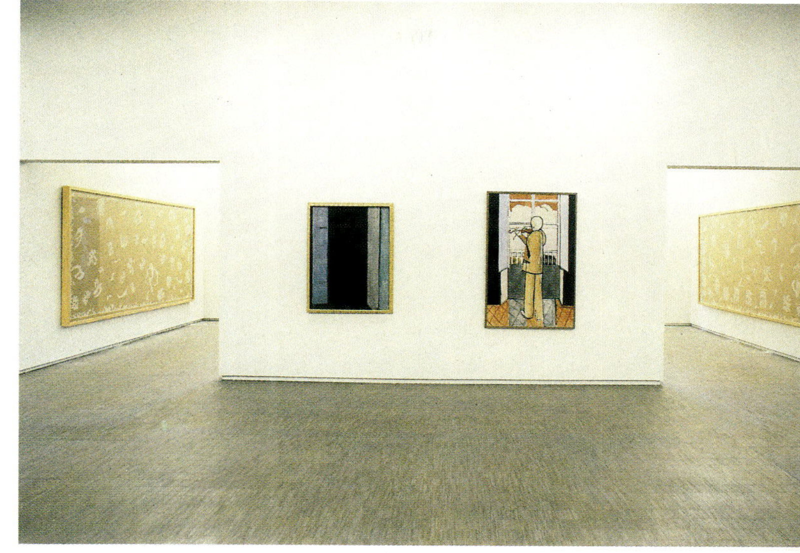

Matisse in figures

Matisse's work is scattered throughout the world in public and private collections. These figures give an idea of how much there is:
- 70 sculptures, including 68 in bronze, 1 in marble and 1 in wood;
- about 800 engravings;
- between 1500 and 2000 paintings;
- countless drawings.

At the end of 1998 the MNAM's collection included:
- 21 bronze sculptures;
- 64 prints;
- 2 works in textile;
- 62 paintings (including the large gouaches);
- 8 wall hangings;
- 122 drawings.

◀ View from the top of the internal escalator in 1977, showing the four bronzes called *The Back*.

▲ The new hanging scheme carried out in 1984 by the Italian architect Gae Aulenti.

Untitled, ►
Medlar Branch (1944).
Pencil or charcoal on paper: 42 x 32 cm.

Drawing is "an act of expression".

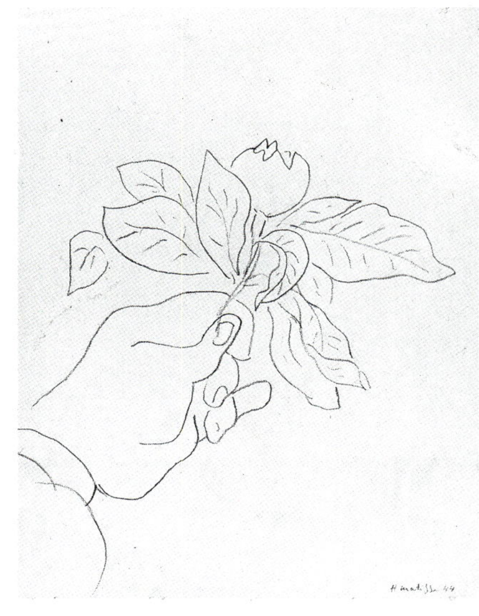

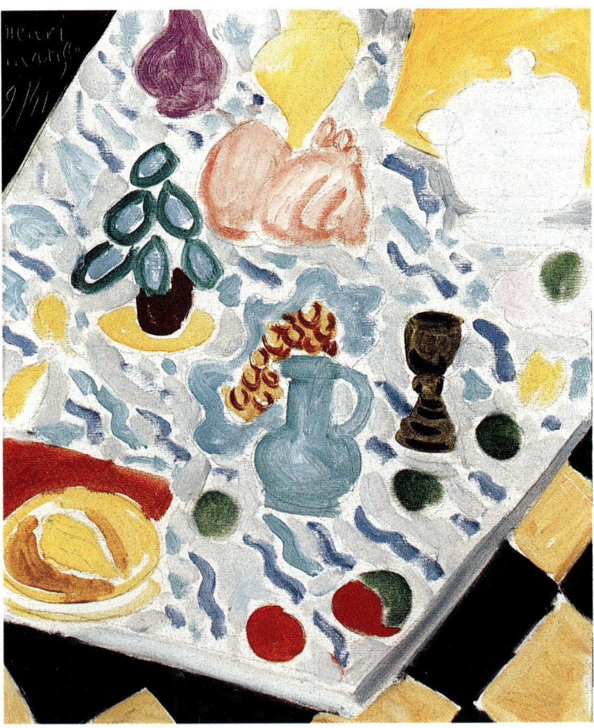

▲
Still-life on a Green Marble Table, September 1941, Nice. Oil on canvas: 46 x 38.5 cm.

Through tight framing, a high angle and the interplay of curves and straight lines, Matisse brings the still, silent world of objects close to us.

Dahlias, Pomegranates and Palm Leaves (1947). ►
Brush and Indian ink on paper: 76.2 x 56.5 cm.

Matisse liked to use his brush to draw as well as to paint. With a brush, "it's always the colour that counts, even when the drawing is made with one continuous line".

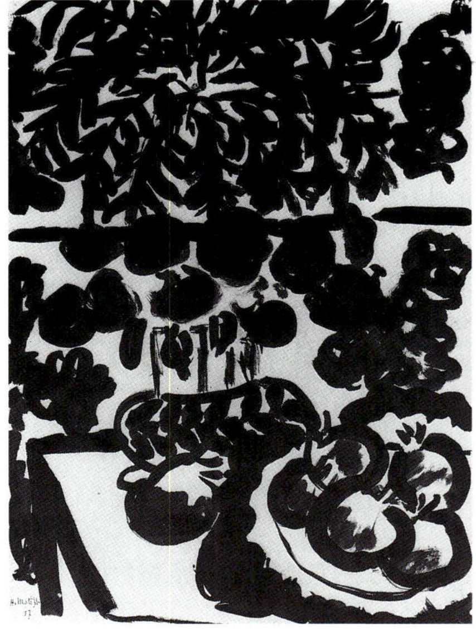

Matisse and the silent life of things

Nothing in Matisse's life destined him to be a painter. He was not one of those precocious geniuses who are born with a paintbrush in their hands. Nor did he grow up in a family of artists, surrounded by works of art. At the age of 20, in 1889, he had never even touched a palette, never visited a museum. Yet he found his true vocation: painting.

He then began a long apprenticeship. No one becomes an artist over-night; Matisse worked endlessly to learn his craft, and he went on learning throughout his whole life. After his death thousands of sketches were found in his spiral-bound notebooks.

To begin with Matisse painted what he saw, the objects around him. Later he said, "For some years I thought that I would paint only still-lifes. It was only after I had shown objects in still-life that I could show the human face." So it was on the motionless world of objects that he first looked with a painter's eye. He never tired of objects. For more than 60 years he painted crockery, objects, fruit and flowers.

Matisse was not interested in faithfully copying nature. For an artist it is not enough just to observe and then to transcribe; the retina, he said, "hides the man". The important thing for a painter was to look with the heart, in order to express on paper or canvas true feelings about reality, to become detached from the appearance of objects. From the beginning Matisse understood that without emotion there is no art.

Still-life, Fruit and Oriental Vase (1941). Pen and Indian ink on paper: 52 x 40 cm.

Matisse's hand, which appears at the bottom, is like his signature. ►

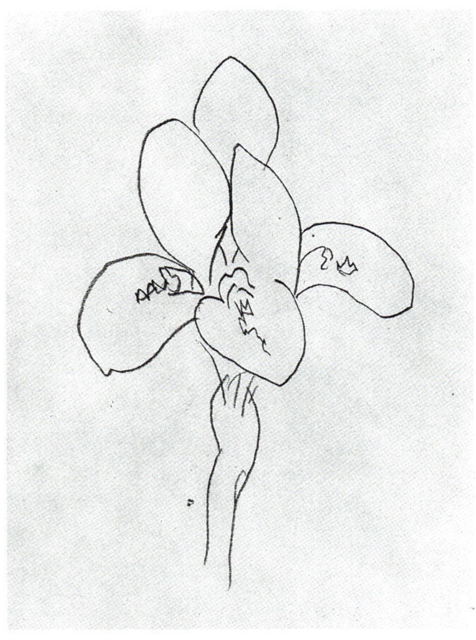

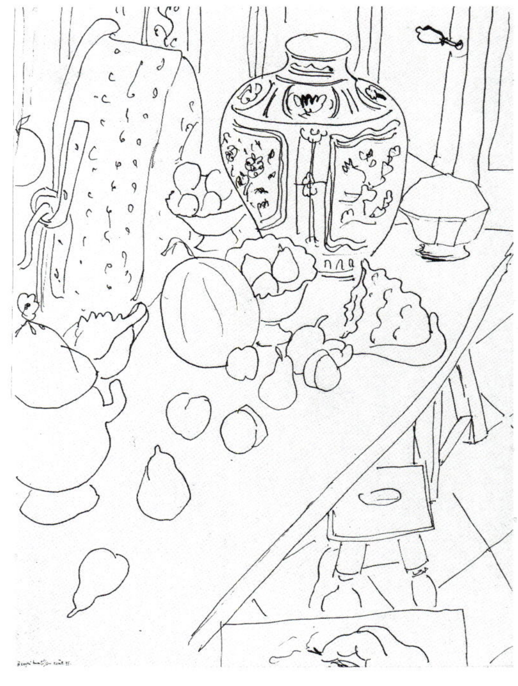

▲
Untitled, *Iris* (1941-42). Pencil on paper (from a sketchbook): 26.9 x 21 cm.

"When you know an object thoroughly, you can catch it with an external line that defines it internally".

Still-life with Magnolia (December 1941), Nice. Oil on canvas: 74 x 101 cm. ►

Matisse made 68 studies before painting this purified image.

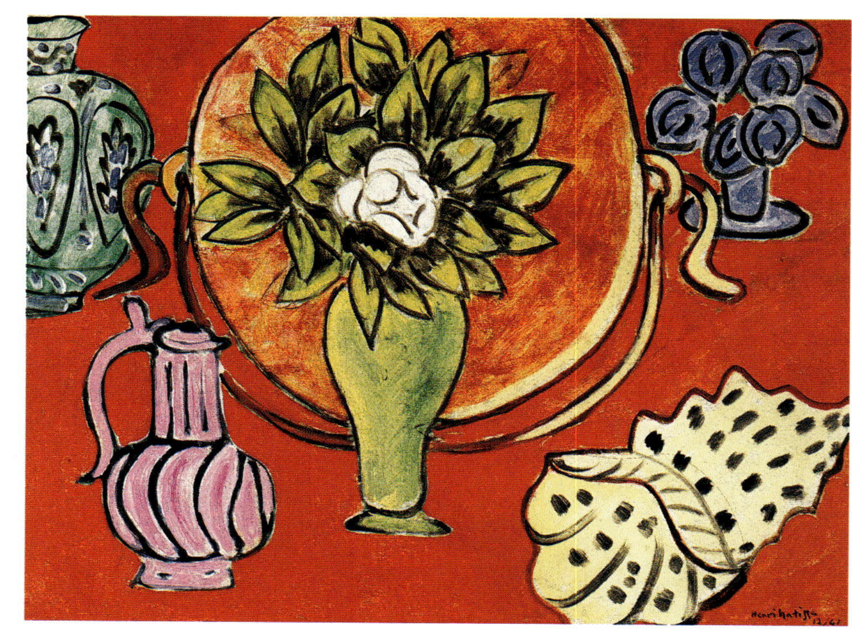

When Matisse looked at a flower, he let himself be carried away by the feelings it awakened in him. It was like setting off on a long journey through virgin forest, he explained. Is this why his countless still-lifes are so vital? "Silent lives" would be a better name; this is in fact the meaning of the German word for still-life, *Stilleben*.
Matisse himself was sometimes surprised at the results of his work: "I put a bunch of flowers on the table. I would like it if when the picture's finished a gardener could recognise all the different kinds of flowers in it; but I don't know what happens along the way – they become girls dancing."

When we look at one of these paintings, we are always surprised and often entranced by the brilliant colours. But Matisse's black and white drawings, whether done in pencil or with a brush, are just as fascinating; what a pure line there is to the iris, and such simplicity in the medlar branch! In his line drawings, Matisse sought to simplify down to the minimum. By always confining himself to the essential lines, he touches us most profoundly.
To make drawings like this succeed, the artist's hand must be supple and as obedient as a slave. The hand is the "continuation of the artist's sensitivity and intelligence", said Matisse. "The servant must not become the mistress". No doubt this is one reason why he chose to paint his own hand so often. But it is probably also an invitation for us to enter his universe, the silent world of creation.

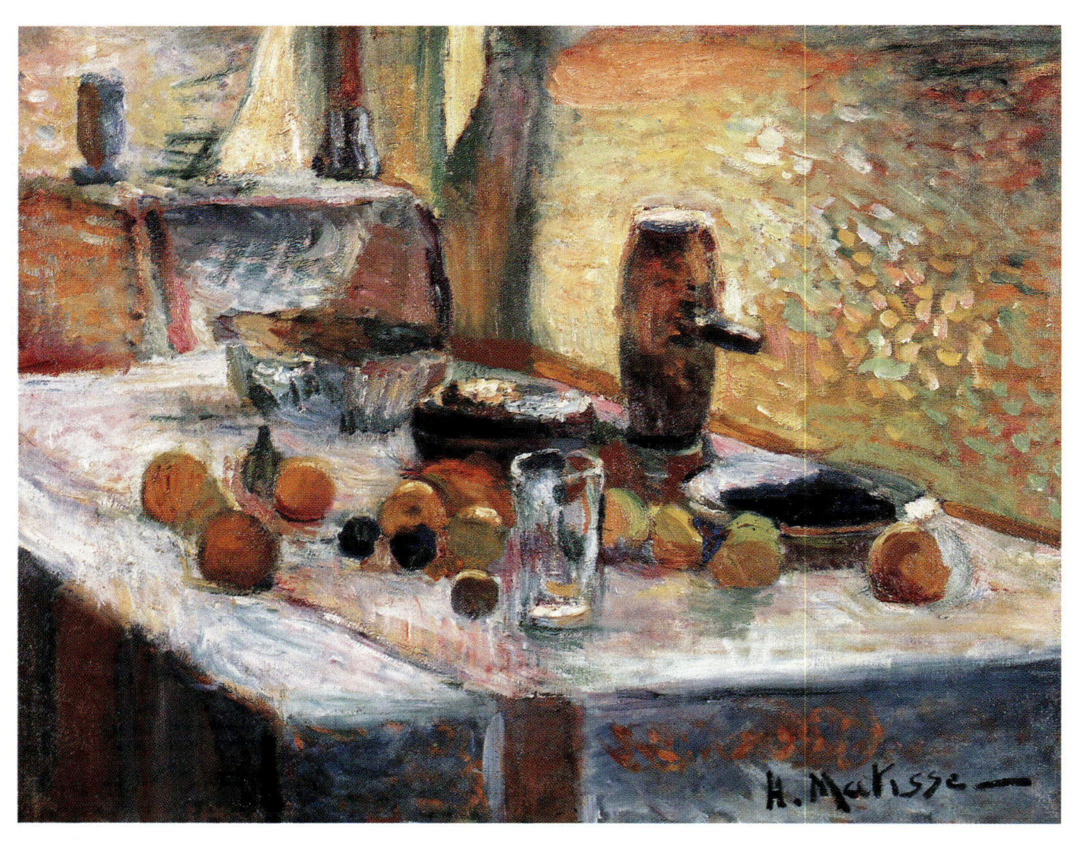

▲
First Orange Still-life
(1899), Toulouse.
Oil on canvas:
56 cm high,
73 cm wide.

FIRST ORANGE STILL-LIFE

1899

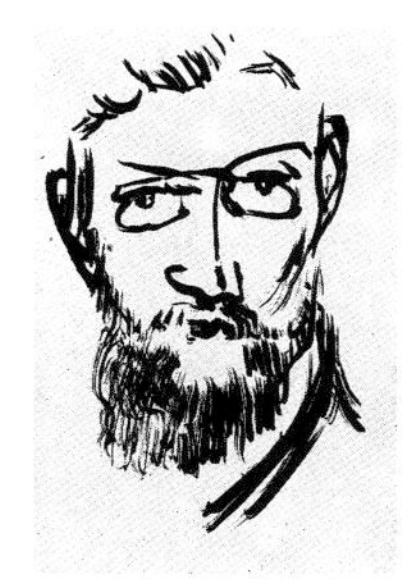

▲
Self-portrait (1900). Brush and Indian ink. Private collection.

This still-life is the work of a young painter still searching for his own style among the works of the great artists of the past. But he has already found the thing that will fascinate him throughout his life: transcribing light.

The title says everything. Here is a still-life which, in keeping with tradition, shows some oranges, a glass, a plate, a large bowl and a coffee pot all arranged on a tablecloth. The composition is simple and rigorous. A rectangular table stands slightly to the left, with its corner towards us. Two other corners are outside the frame. The impression of depth is created by this interplay of diagonal lines.

A painter is entirely present in his first pictures.
Matisse.

reflecting the light

The eye is held by an intense light. It comes from the left, bathing the table and right wall in its orange tones. Matisse has chosen a range of pale, warm colours. His brush strokes are sometimes light and fluid, sometimes dense and thick, the variation betraying his hesitations and choices; they caress the fruit – the oranges – in a circular movement in which some of the shapes dissolve. And the right wall, for example, is painted in skipping strokes, as though the painter were intoxicated by so much light. Matisse painted this still-life in Toulouse. It was the first of its kind. The theme of orange – both the colour and the fruit – was to recur throughout his entire work.

a painter of the 19th or the 20th century?

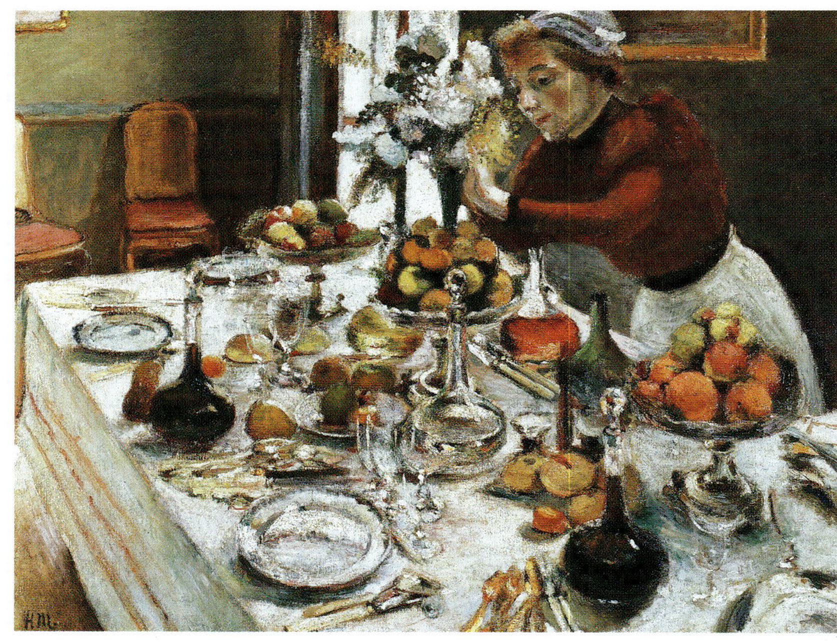

▲ *Dinner Table* (1897). Oil on canvas: 100 x 131 cm. Private collection.

A year before he started work on the *First Orange Still-life*, Matisse was already using orange, a warm colour, to set off the white of the tablecloth.

Apples, pears and apricots
Why do 17th-century still-lifes show summer and winter fruits together? Because they have a symbolic role: apples and pears signify forbidden fruit, cherries the fruit of paradise. In those days a painting had to be both beautiful and symbolic.

Matisse was born in Picardy, a region of France bordering on Belgium and Flanders. It was there, in the 17th century, that the first still-lifes were painted. In painting pictures like *Dinner Table*, Matisse was paying homage to his Flemish masters. In his turn, he showed gleaming plates and the light reflected off glasses and carafes, surrounded by a profusion of fruit: "the substance of things", he called it.

heir to a tradition

Not content to imitate, Matisse was an innovator; for example, he put a living person in this still-life. The servant leaning over the flowers recalls a different kind of painting – Realism – which had appeared 50 years earlier.
Like Courbet, the first French realist painter, and Manet, who was 37 years older than Matisse, he painted a face that is neither beautiful nor ugly,

◀ **Edouard Manet** (1832-83), *Still-life, Fruits on a Table* (1869). Oil on canvas: 45 x 73.5 cm. Musée d'Orsay, Paris.

Copying: a learning exercise
Until the end of the 19th century, young painters trained in the studio of a recognised artist, who guided and supervised their work. Copying pictures by the masters was one of the classic exercises, like life drawing.

solemn nor dramatic. He painted an expression taken from real life.

Another striking aspect of the *First Orange Still-life* is the vibrant strokes of light colour, brilliant and luminous in tone. How can we not think of the Impressionists who had brought about a revolution in painting 20 years earlier? With their pale palettes and pure colours, they were trying to capture the quality of light at one particular moment.

Matisse uses a very similar technique, but he is not trying to convey "a fleeting sensation". He wants to paint his emotion – a lasting emotion. This is why he turned first to the old masters.

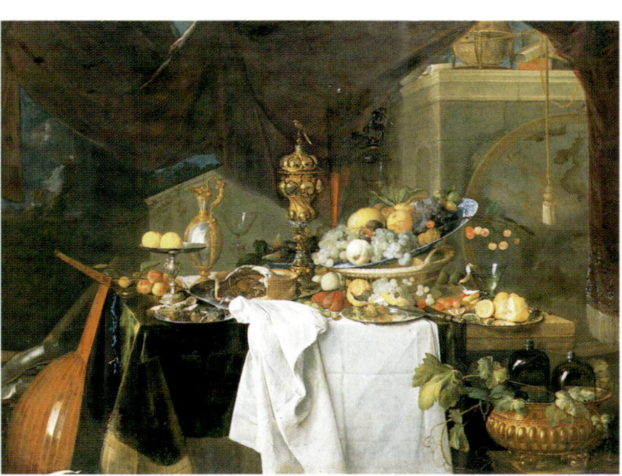

◀ **Jan Davidsz de Heem** (1606-84), *The Dessert* (1640). Oil on canvas: 149 x 203 cm. The Louvre, Paris.

Matisse liked simple still-lifes, but he also admired this painting from the 17th century of the remains of a sumptuous feast, which he copied at the Louvre in his youth.

how did Matisse learn to paint?

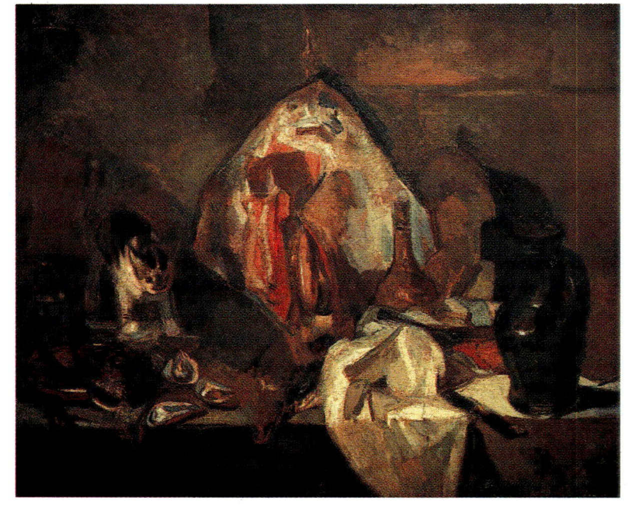

◄ *Copy after Chardin's* The Skate (1894-1901). Oil on canvas: 115 x 142 cm. Musée Matisse, Le Cateau-Cambrésis.

"I began with Davidsz de Heem's still-life. Then I tried to paint *The Skate* in sections." Matisse.

In 1890 Matisse was working as a lawyer in Saint-Quentin. While recovering from appendicitis, he drew to pass the time. Was it chance or fate? He just discovered painting. Like Van Gogh and Gauguin, he gave up everything to follow his vocation.

conventional painting? absolutely not!

I add colour until it resembles the original. Matisse never forgot these words of Chardin's.

What he most wanted was to get a classical training. He enrolled at the Académie Julien in Paris, where he was taught by William Bouguereau and Gabriel Ferrier, who were famous painters of the time.

What a disappointment! He was criticised for knowing nothing about perspective, for rubbing his drawing out with his finger rather than using a rag, for starting with the model's hand instead of the head...

The following year, Matisse enrolled at the École des Beaux-Arts. Same reception, same disappointment.

Finally he managed to get into the studio of Gustave Moreau. There at last he met a master who respected his personality, without obliging him to paint in a particular way, and who threw open the doors of art to

Copying: a way to make a living
Many painters, even today, make copies, which they sell to art lovers. Some become professional copyists. Others, like Matisse in his early days, copy paintings in order to earn a living and to buy brushes, canvas and paint.

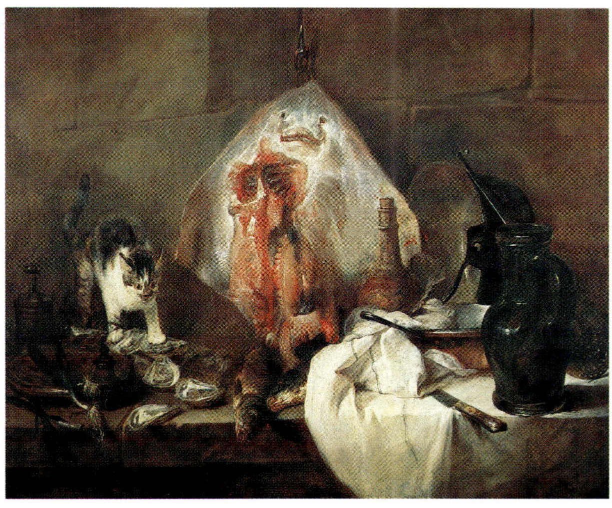

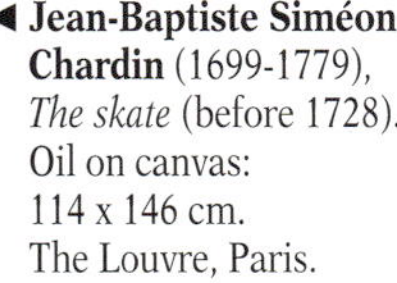

◄ **Jean-Baptiste Siméon Chardin** (1699-1779), *The skate* (before 1728). Oil on canvas: 114 x 146 cm. The Louvre, Paris.

In the Louvre, Matisse mainly studied the paintings of Chardin, particularly *The Skate*. It was this picture that ensured Chardin's admission to the Academy of painting.

William Bouguereau ► (1825-1905), *The Birth of Venus* (1879). Oil on canvas: 300 x 218 cm. Musée d'Orsay, Paris.

A perfect example of the overdone, artificial art known as "kitsch". It was in the studio of this academic painter that Matisse learned just what not to do!

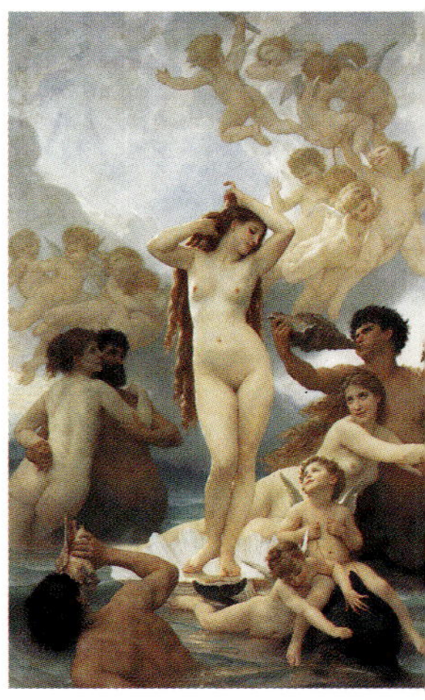

him. He discovered the treasures of the Louvre, which he studied by copying them: Raphael, Poussin, de Heem and above all Chardin, whom he admired as a colourist.

Matisse learnt a great deal from these years of study and adopted the dark colours of the great masters. When he went south, however, to Toulouse, home to the family of his wife, Amélie Parayre, he left these dark colours behind him. "The quest for colour", he acknowledged, "did not come to me from studying other painters, but from the outside, that is, from a revelation of light in nature". The man of the north had just discovered the light of the Midi.

when the sun plays a part

Matisse's *First Orange Still-life* marks a turning point. In it the painter is freeing himself from what he has learnt, without yet having truly found his own language. Would Matisse be the painter of form and line, which give structure to the picture, or of the vibrant light that makes structure dissolve?

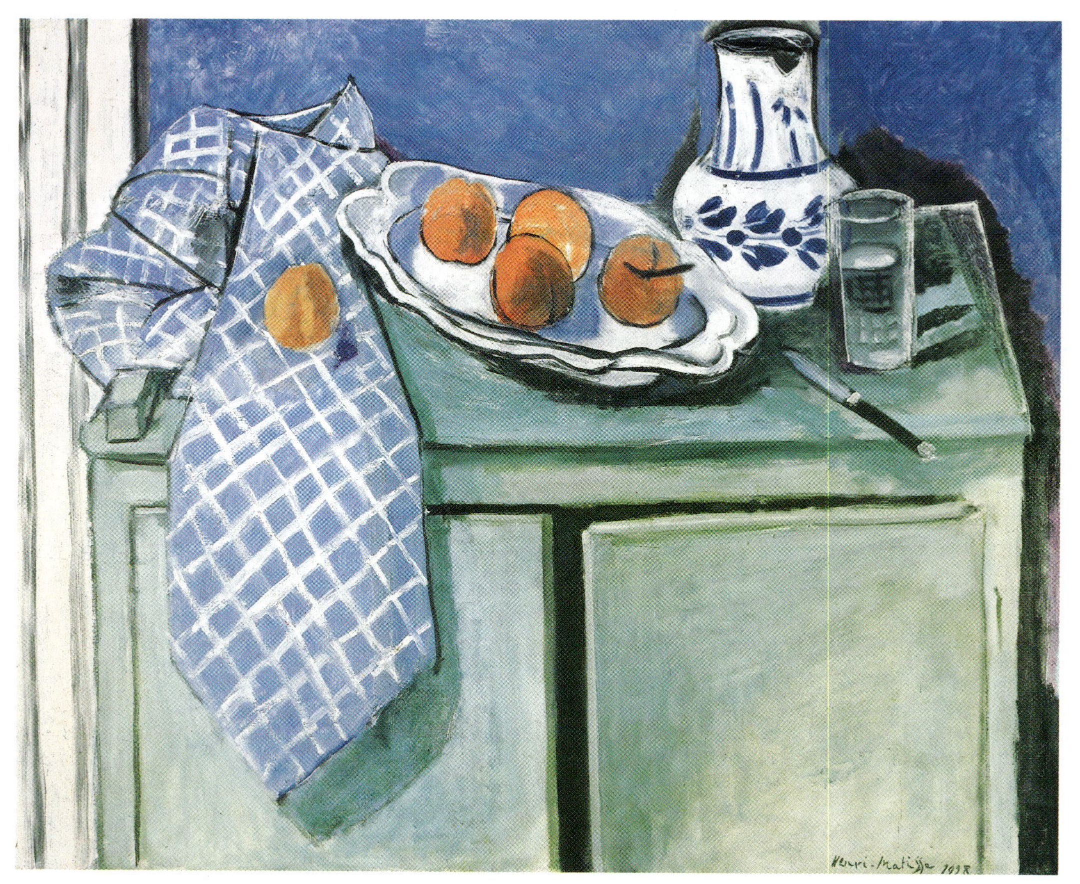

▲
Still-life on a Green Sideboard (July 1928),
Nice.
Oil on canvas:
81.5 cm high,
100 cm wide.

STILL-LIFE ON A GREEN SIDEBOARD

1928

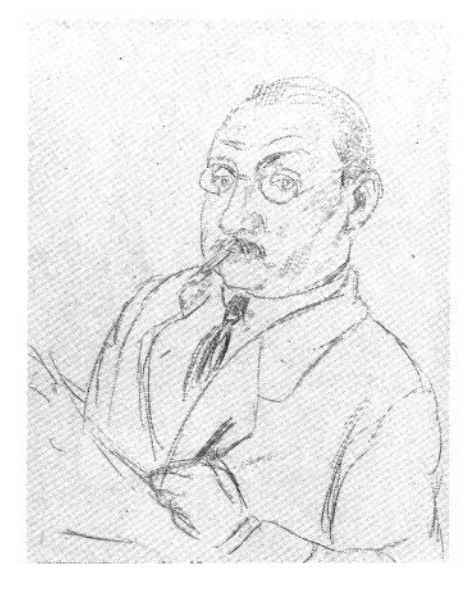

▲
Self-portrait (1927). Graphite pencil on paper: 22.7 x 17.4 cm.

Nearly thirty years after *First Orange Still-life*, Matisse was still working on the theme that obsessed him; the objects – oranges, a tablecloth, a jug, a glass – are just the same, yet everything has changed.

From 1921 onwards, Matisse spent almost all his time in the brilliant light of Nice, which he so loved. He eventually found a large studio on the Place Charles-Félix, and painted the walls blue, perhaps so they would merge with the sky. Nearly 30 years had passed between the *First Orange Still-life* and *Still-life on a Green Sideboard*, and in that time Matisse had become famous.

In still-life, copying objects is nothing; the aim is to convey the emotions they awaken. The emotion of the whole picture, the relationship between the objects, and the specific nature of each object, modified by its relationships with the others [...]. Everything is all twisted together, like a rope or a snake. Matisse, noted by Sarah Stein, 1908.

the triumph of orange

The composition is dominated by four oranges on a dish, next to a blue-and-white jug and a glass of water. Yet the sideboard takes up a lot of space; it fills three-quarters of the picture and it figures in the title. Behind this sea-green mass, the blue wall holds the eye. All the objects seem to bump against the edges of the painting. Only the tablecloth and, particularly, the knife and the open door open up the space towards the spectator. Matisse is not trying to suggest the volume of the objects; he paints using flat colour. Here he no longer bathes his picture in a warm light. Instead he plays on the contrast between cold colours (green and blue) and the warmth of orange. Orange was to become Matisse's emblem; what other fruit bears the name of its colour?

must the rules of perspective be obeyed?

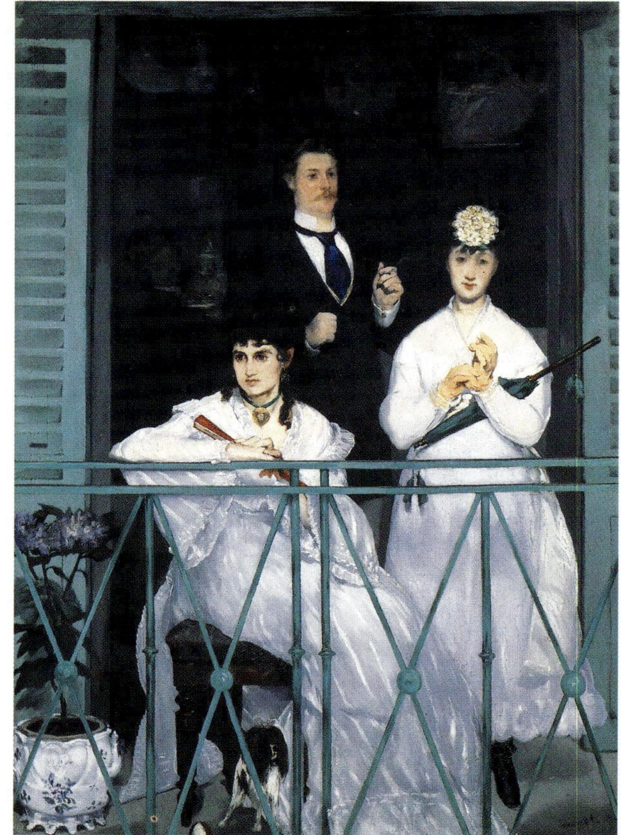

◀ **Edouard Manet** (1832-83), *The Balcony* (1868-69). Oil on canvas: 170 x 124.5 cm. Musée d'Orsay, Paris.

Like Matisse, Manet admired the work of the Spanish painter Goya, who inspired him to paint this work. The blue-green of the balcony and shutters is similar to the colour of Matisse's sideboard. Painted in flat colour and without any shading, this blue-green was critised by Manet's contemporaries, who dismissed him as a "house painter".

Matisse's oranges
Every year I send him a box of oranges and Picasso displays it in his studio, saying to his visitors, "Look, those are Matisse's oranges". And no one dares to eat them.
Brassaï, 1982.

Is this still-life constructed according to classical norms? Apparently yes. Geometric lines give it rigour and simplicity. The opening between the doors and the shadows under the dish, on the sideboard, behind the glass and on the wall all obey strict rules of perspective. Matisse seems to want to keep as close as possible to what his eye sees when painting objects.

And yet, we do not see any shadow of a shadow on the tablecloth, which is almost uniformly blue and white. And why is its chequered pattern so regular, although the lines are seen arranged in checks horizontally on the sideboard and diagonally hanging over the door? The sideboard doesn't work either; according to the laws of perspective, the two sides of the top should be almost parallel, but joining at a vanishing point in the

Basket of Oranges, (1912). Oil on canvas: 94 x 83 cm. Musée Picasso, Paris. ▶

Picasso, Matisse's friend and rival, was not only a great painter but also a great collector. He bought this picture in 1944, during World War II. He particularly admired its rigorous composition and the way it reinvented space.

A fruit of light
If Henri Matisse's work can be compared to anything, it would have to be the orange. Like oranges, Henri Matisse's work is a brilliant fruit of light.
Guillaume Apollinaire, Preface to the catalogue of the Matisse-Picasso Exhibition, Paris, 1918.

far distance. And what about the solitary orange which is not actually resting on the tablecloth? It is no longer an orange but represents a three-dimensional "coloured shape" suspended in mid-air.

no more optical illusions!

Matisse said, and went on saying, painting reality did not interest him. "In modern art, it's indisputably to Cézanne that I owe most", he wrote in his *Notes d'un peintre* ("Notes of a Painter"). Like Cézanne, he first submitted to his model, observing it attentively, then he translated it into paint, simplifying as he did so. This is why Matisse did not bother with perspective, which only serves to fool the spectator's eye. To express what he feels, he needs to forget theories and techniques and to listen to his heart beating in response to objects.

Paul Cézanne
(1839-1906),
Still-life, Apples and Oranges
(c. 1895-1900).
Oil on canvas:
74 x 93 cm.
Musée d'Orsay, Paris.

Matisse regarded Cézanne as the "master of us all". What a lot of similarities there are here between the works of the two painters: interplaying straight and curving lines, a jug, a ceramic dish and round fruit.
▼

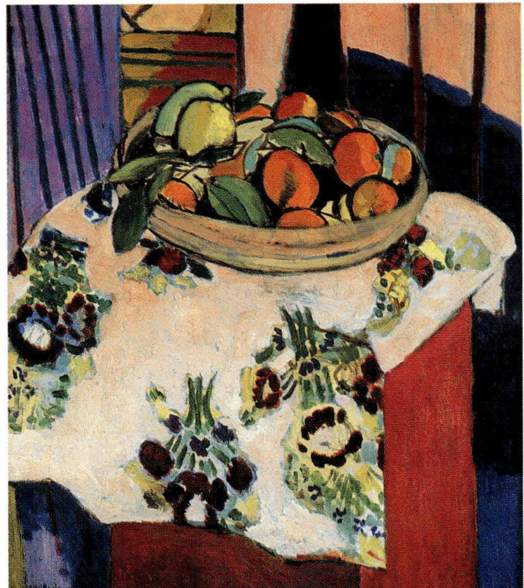

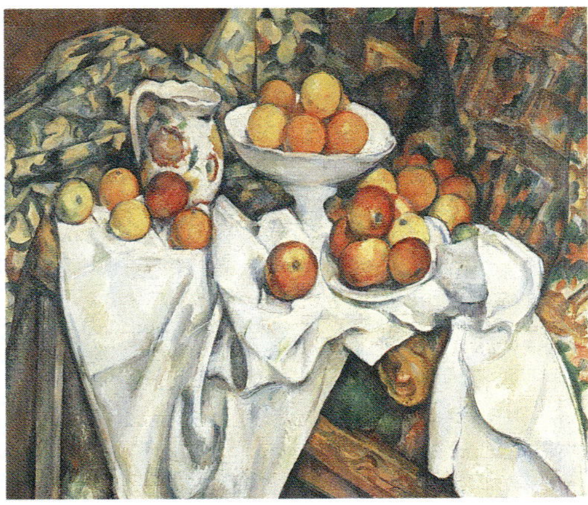

why do the doors open on to nothing?

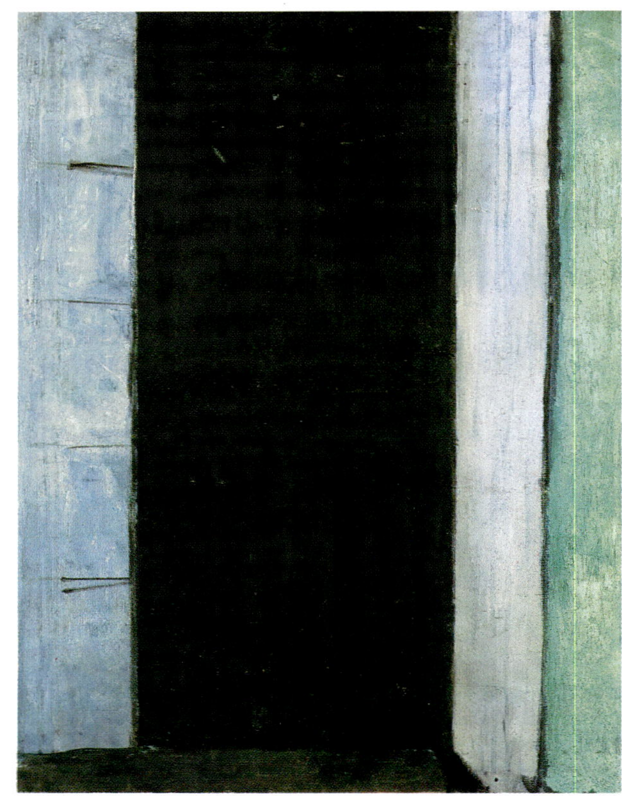

◀ *French Window at Collioure* (1914). Oil on canvas: 116 x 89 cm.

Painted at the start of World War I, this open door, hiding more than it shows, has been interpreted as a symbol of a dark future.

We could have felt excluded from this picture's world of lines. To allow us to enter it, Matisse opens the doors of the sideboard, points the knife towards us and lets part of the tablecloth hang. He takes his inspiration from the great still-life painters, Chardin, Manet and Cézanne.

The classical painter's tricks
Invented in the Renaissance (in the 16th century), perspective makes it possible to create an impression of depth in only two dimensions. Lines that are parallel in reality appear to converge in the distance at a "vanishing point". In addition, to give a sense of volume to an object, the artist grades the colour, moving from dark in the foreground to light farther away. This creates the effect of "relief".

behind the door...

The open doors reveal a dark interior, reminiscent of an earlier painting by Matisse, *French Window at Collioure*. Already there is the same cold harmony of blue and green and rigorous geometrical construction. The opening of the French window is suggested by a small diagonal line at the bottom of the picture. It is this that justifies the wide, dark, vertical band, the subject of the composition itself. The austerity of this picture, which is unique in Matisse's work, surprised his contemporaries. Painted in 1914, at the start of World War I, it shows the painter's anxiety in the face of a dark and uncertain future.

The Poetics of Space
In this book, the philosopher Gaston Bachelard analyses our private spaces – such as houses, corners, wardrobes, chests – and the effects they have on us. In particular he discusses the fascination of the half-open door, which stimulates our imaginations.

... a secret garden

In 1928 the opening of the sideboard does not cause anxiety. Its chief role is to draw the eye. If we follow the painter's lead, push the door and enter the picture, Matisse will show us his secret world.
This, at any rate, is the artist's idea; two years before his death he told his friend André Verdet, "It's by entering the object that you enter your own skin [...] I had to make this budgerigar out of coloured paper. So I became a budgerigar. And I found myself in the work."

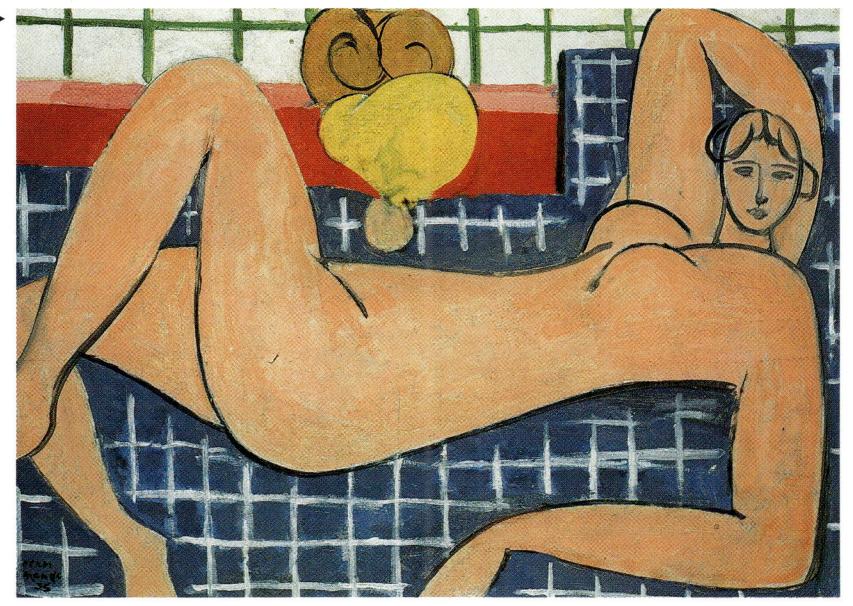

Pink Nude (1935). Oil on canvas: 66 x 92 cm. Museum of Art, Baltimore, Cone Collection.

From still-life, Matisse moved naturally to painting women. Here orange has given way to a magnificent pink nude. Here again we can see his liking for a pattern of white checks on blue, which recurs frequently.

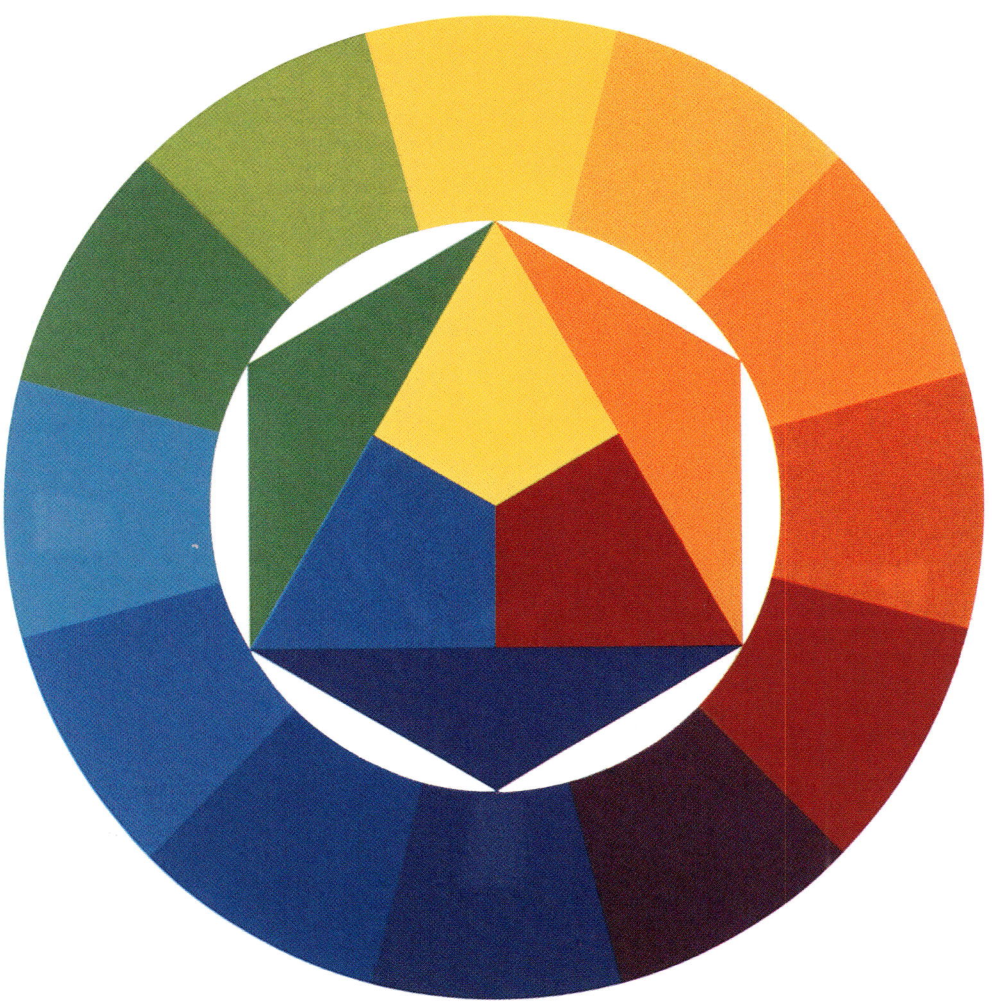

▲
Itten's chromatic circle

The Swiss painter Johannes Itten (1888-1967) wanted to arrange colours in relation to each other. So he devised a circle; at the centre are the three primary colours, which cannot be obtained by mixing: red, yellow and blue. Mixing the primary colours, two by two, produces three secondary colours, orange, green and violet, which surround the basic triangle.
The hexagon this forms shows that each primary colour is diametrically opposed to what is known as its complementary colour: green and red, orange and blue, violet and yellow. These are all surrounded by a second circle, split into 12 parts, which contains both the primary and secondary colours and intermediate colours (each obtained by mixing a primary and a secondary colour together).

The only disadvantage of Itten's chromatic circle is that it does not include black, white or the brown tones (the neutral colours).

Matisse, or colour unleashed

"I feel through colour, so it's through colour that my canvas will always be organised," Matisse told one of his friends in 1943. Colours are substances first and foremost. In the Middle Ages artists made their own colours by grinding up stone, earth or plants and mixing them with a liquid. Blue, for example, was made from a powdered semi-precious stone, lapis lazuli.

But, as we know today, colour is also a very complex physical phenomenon, indissociable from light. The British mathematician and scientist Isaac Newton (1643-1727) was the first to split light. He used a prism to replicate what happens when light passes through a drop of water – a rainbow appears.
In the 19th century the German writer Goethe developed a theory of colour. He described what the eye sees, but also gave each colour a symbolic, almost magical value. For him green symbolised sensuality, purple imagination, yellow reason and blue understanding.

Since then, scientists, philosophers and, above all, painters have developed new theories. That of the Swiss painter Johannes Itten is the best known today. In *The Art of Colour*, published in 1961, he established the physical laws of colour and in the chromatic circle he set out the primary, secondary, complementary and intermediate colours.

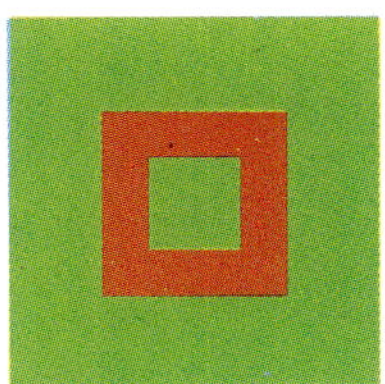

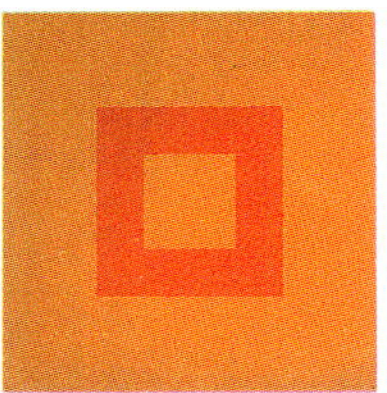

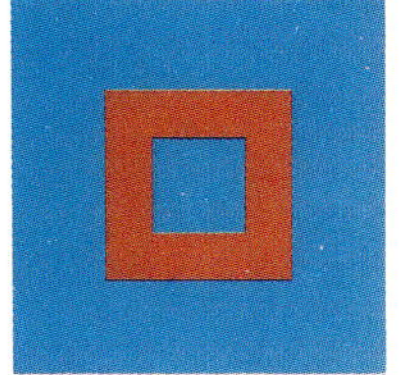

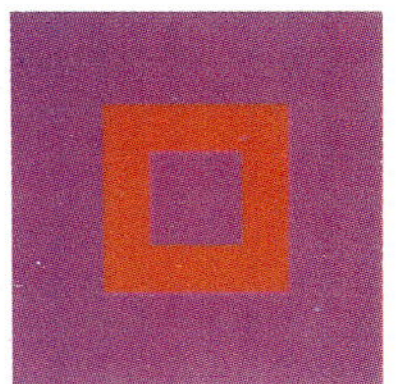

▲
Colour proximities

A colour looks different depending on the colour next to it.

Portrait of Madame Matisse, called *The Green Stripe* (1905).

Oil on canvas: 40.5 x 32.5 cm. Statens Museum for Kunst, Copenhagen.

► 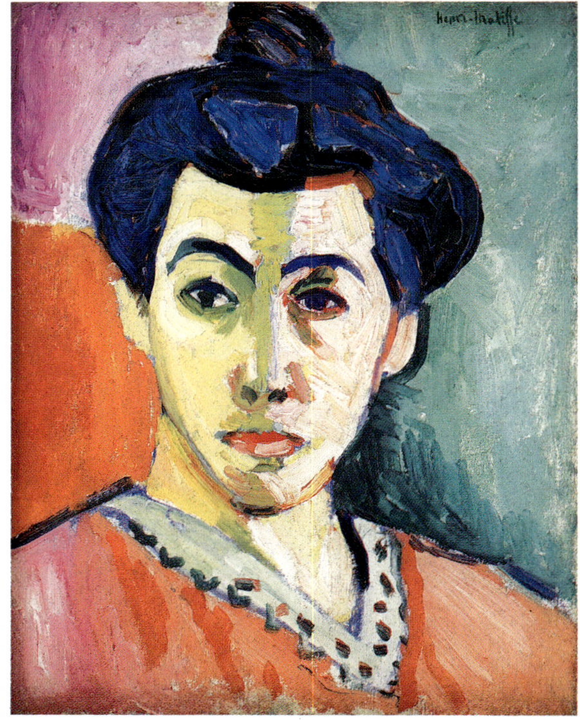

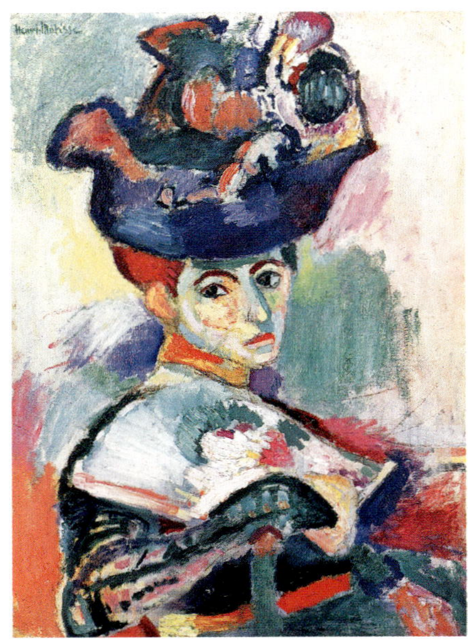

▲
Woman in a Hat (Madame Matisse) (1905).
Oil on canvas: 80.6 x 59.7 cm.
Museum of Modern Art, San Francisco.

With this picture Matisse became the undisputed leader of Fauvism.

Blue Nude (Memory of Biskra) (1907).
Oil on canvas: 92 x 140 cm.
Museum of Art, Baltimore, Cone Collection. ►

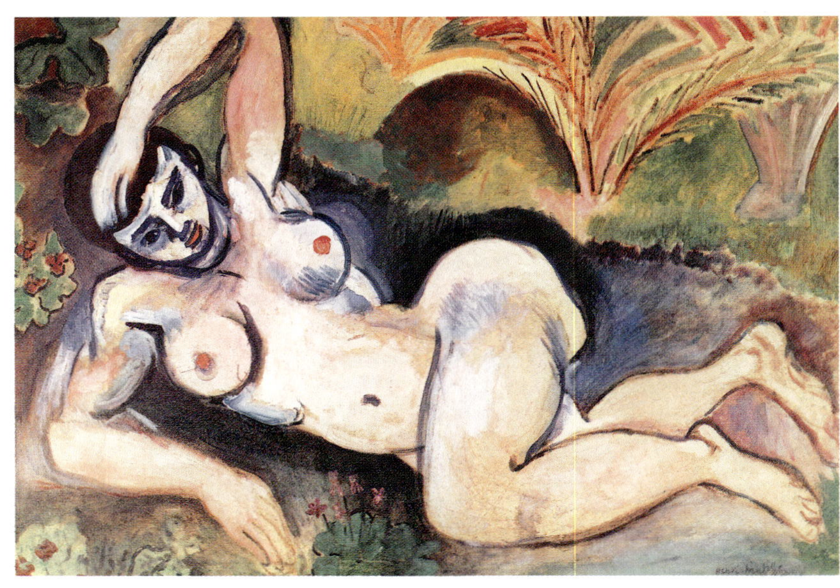

This *Blue Nude* ended burnt at the stake ...

Matisse was a conscientious student who learnt all the theories. Then he tried to forget them. For what really matters is to have a gift and to let it speak. In 1908 he wrote to Sarah Stein, "The choice of my colours is not based on any scientific theory; it is based on observation, feeling, on the expression of my sensibility".
By starting from scratch like this, Matisse exploded the scientific theories. At the dawn of the 20th century, he discovered the true expressive force of colour – as long as it is pure. "In painting, colours only have their power and eloquence when they are used in a pure state". By using colour, not to imitate or to transcribe nature but to express his emotions, Matisse opened up a new path to 20th-century painters.

A great innovation rarely leaves the art world indifferent. In 1905, when Matisse exhibited his *Woman in a Hat* at the Autumn Salon, it caused a scandal. Wild beasts, or "*fauves*" was how a furious critic described the painter and his friends Henri Manguin, André Derain, Louis Valtat and Georges Rouault. In 1913 the art lovers' fury had not calmed down; at the Armory Show exhibition in Chicago, one of Matisse's Fauvist pictures, *Blue Nude (Memory of Biskra),* was judged "indecent and epileptic" to the extent that it was brandished in the streets before being burnt. And yet, the exhibition of some 1,600 paintings included some extraordinary Picassos.

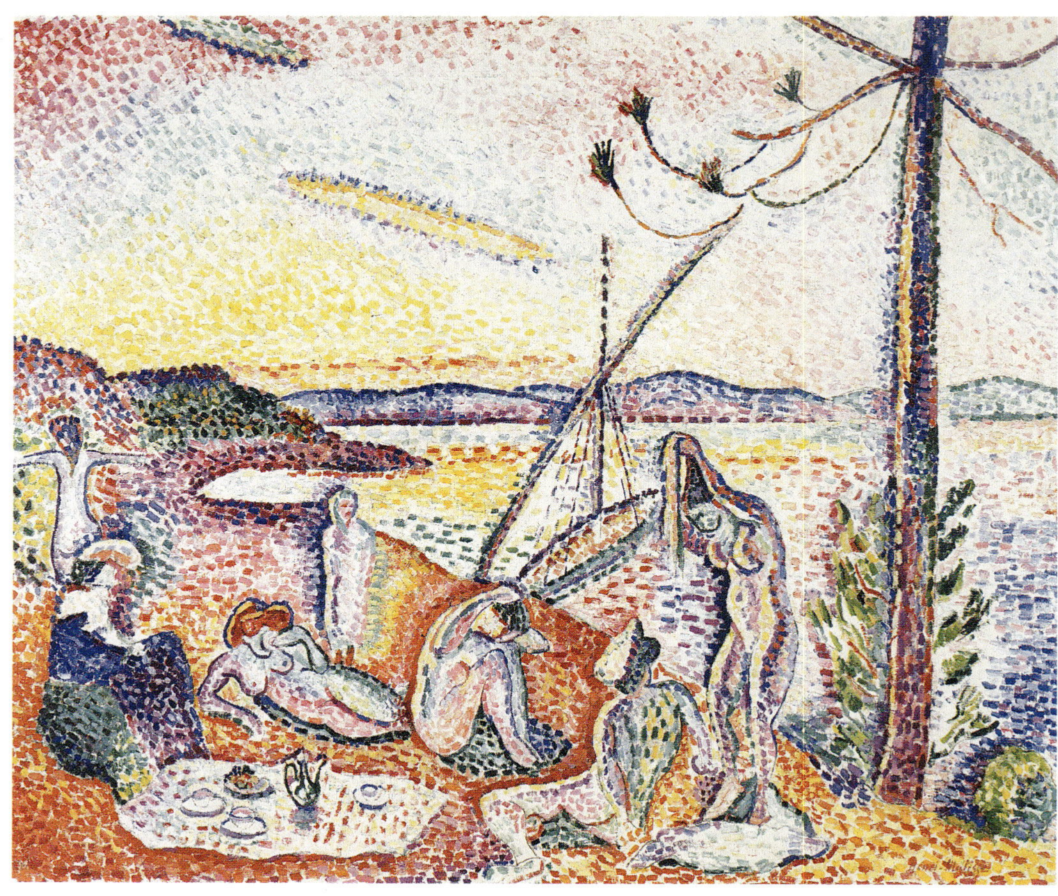

▲
Luxe, calme et volupté ("Luxury, calm and sensuality") (autumn 1904), Paris.
Oil on canvas: 98.5 cm high, 118.8 cm wide.
MNAM collection, lent to the Musée d'Orsay, Paris.

Don't look for this picture at the Musée National d'Art Moderne, which owns it. It is on show at the Musée d'Orsay in Paris, where it is held on trust as a transitional work poised between 19th- and 20th-century art.

LUXE, CALME ET VOLUPTÉ

1904

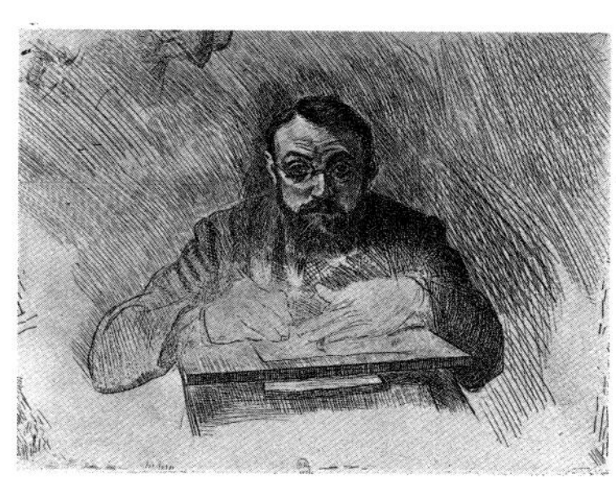

▲ *Self-portrait*, Henri Matisse engraving (1903). Dry-point: 15 x 19.9 cm. Bibliothèque Nationale, Paris.

A classic seaside holiday scene. What is less classical is the technique Matisse uses: why does he speckle his canvas with small strokes, like a Pointillist?

By the sea, in the Gulf of Saint-Tropez, six women and a child are finishing a picnic. Only one woman is dressed, the others are naked; they have come out of the water to sunbathe. The child stands apart. His face and silhouette are undefined, as though he were seen against the light. As in a photo, each woman is caught in a different, natural pose. But none of their faces can be distinguished.

all the colours of the rainbow

Once again it is the luminosity of the scene that is surprising. Matisse treats everything in the same way, and with the same attention: the pine with its thin, dancing branches, the sailing boat below it, the sky with its clouds.
He bathes everything – landscape and bodies – in the same light, in so many colours – light and sharp, warm in the foreground, cold in the distance and in the shade. On the beach red is placed next to yellow, then blue, with effects of violet; the blue, carmine and yellow of the sky contaminate a cloud, flood into the sea and spread forwards like fire, as far as the pine's trunk. A real firework of a painting, but one that does not explode.

why little dots every-where?

What patience it must take to put so many little dots of pure colour next to each other! They all go in a particular direction: horizontal for the water, which is dead calm; vertical for the trunk, standing straight upright; diagonal for the sky, a rain of light. Here and there the dots sometimes merge, for example on the women's rounded bodies. Why did Matisse choose such a demanding technique?

He got it from Paul Signac, first by reading one of his works then, more importantly, by getting to know him in 1904. That was a year of upheaval for Matisse. He wanted to paint in more luminous colours so that he could express his feelings better, but without exposing them too much. Might the solution lie with Pointillism, or Divisionism, invented by Signac? Like all avant-garde painters, Matisse showed his work in the Salon

Study of a Pine (1904). Pencil on two sheets of paper: 32 x 34 cm. Musée Matisse, Nice.

One of the studies drawn by Matisse.

▼

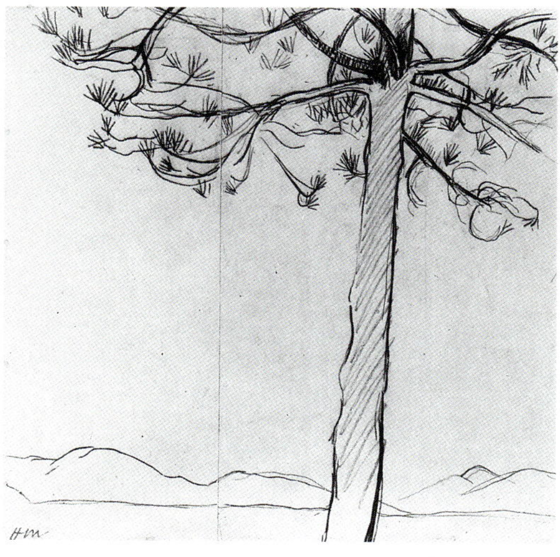

Paul Signac (1863-1935). *The Red Buoy* (1895). Oil on canvas: 81 x 65 cm. Musée d'Orsay, Paris.

This red buoy is floating in the harbour at Saint-Tropez, where Signac was working on light. He used pure colours, which he did not mix on either the palette or the canvas. He juxtaposed them in small dots.

▼

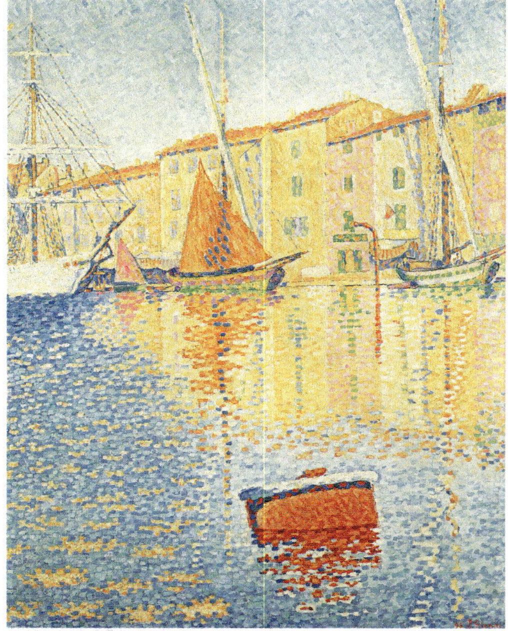

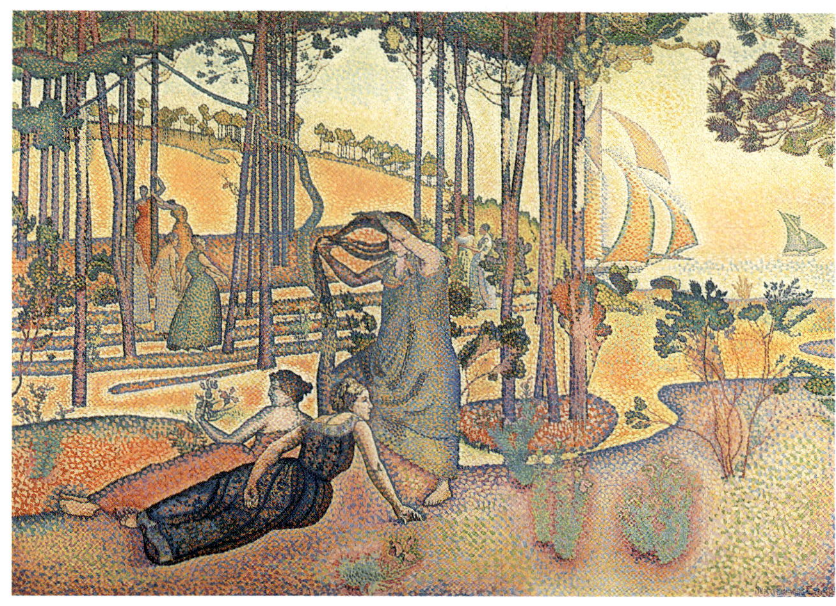

▲
Edmond Cross
(1856-1910),
Evening Air (1893-94).
Oil on canvas:
115 x 163 cm.
Musée d'Orsay, Paris.

This picture resembles *Luxe, calme et volupté* in so many ways: it has a similar theme and a composition based on horizontal, vertical and curved lines; even the women's poses are similar, particularly those who are brushing their long hair.

Pointillism conquers Europe
Divisionism, or Pointillism, quickly won over Gauguin and Van Gogh. The movement spread to Holland with Toorop, to Belgium with Van de Velde and Van Rysselberghe, to Italy with Pelizza da Volpido and Segantini. In 1905 Matisse opened the way to the Fauvists – Derain, Vlaminck and Rouault – then to the optical Cubists – Metzinger and Robert Delaunay – and the Futurists – Gino Severini and Giacomo Balla.

des Indépendants (Independents' Exhibition) run by Signac. The two men became friends and Signac invited Matisse to his house in Saint-Tropez for the summer. Since his first encounter with the light of the Midi in 1898 in Toulouse, Matisse had been unable to live without the sun. He did not, of course, go for a holiday; he wanted to work with Signac to find a new way to paint.

inspiration under the sun

Matisse now had three children and took Amélie and Pierre with him. One day, when he was using them as models for a little seaside scene called *Teatime*, he began to dream of a larger composition. Seeing *Evening Air* by Signac's friend Edmond Cross, his dream took shape. Matisse set to work.

birth of a new school: Divisionism

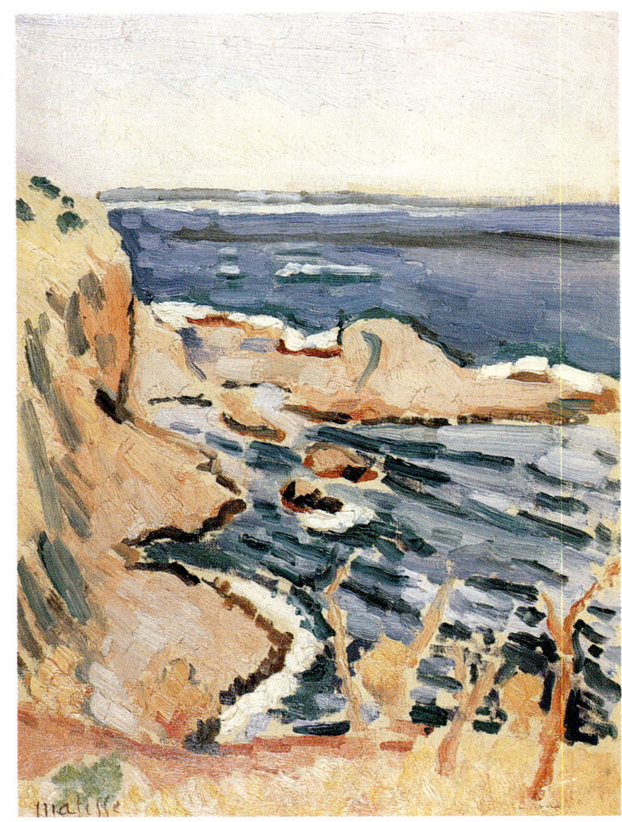

◄ *Seascape: La Moulade* (summer 1905), Collioure. Oil on card: 31.5 x 24 cm. Private collection.

A year after he painted *Luxe, calme et volupté*, Matisse's brush strokes became elongated so that in this painting he could contrast the horizontals of the sea with the verticals of the cliff edge.

In Saint-Tropez, Matisse kept working on his large seaside composition. As usual he began with a drawing and sketches, rough at first, then more detailed. Then he began doing studies, painting with fluid strokes. He tried out the Divisionist technique, but it did not satisfy him. Although the colours were pure, they had no brilliance. Besides, splitting them up like that broke up the picture's forms; the surface shimmered and vibrated. But Matisse did not have time to finish the painting.

Good news was waiting for him in Paris. The administration of the Ecole des Beaux-Arts was buying his copy of Raphael's *Balthasar Castiglione*. Excellent for his finances!

Matisse went to two big exhibitions: that of Puvis de Chavannes, whose peaceful grandeur he much admired, and

Neo-Impressionism
This movement followed that of the Impressionists. It was led by Georges Seurat (1859-91). The Neo-Impressionists used pure colours, juxtaposing them with small strokes on the canvas – hence the term Pointillism or Divisionism. They are united only by the eye of the onlooker. The colours thus seen are purer than when they are mixed on the palette or canvas. This technique was based on various scientific theories, particularly that of French chemist Eugène Chevreul.

My child, my sister,
imagine the sweetness
of going there to live
together!
To love at leisure,
to love and to die
in the land which
resembles you!
The watery suns
of these bleary skies
have to my mind the
mysterious charms
of your treacherous
eyes,
shining through
their tears.

There, all is order
and beauty,
luxury, calm and
sensuality.

"Invitation to a Journey" from *Les Fleurs du mal* ("The Flowers of evil") by Charles Baudelaire.

◄ **André Derain** (1880-1954), *Boats at Collioure* (1905). Oil on canvas: 47 x 46 cm. Staatsgalerie, Stuttgart.

In Collioure Matisse continued his researches into light and colour in the company of Derain, who shared his interest in the Divisionist technique but painted with larger, squarer strokes.

more importantly that of Cézanne. Admiring Cézanne's *Bathers*, Matisse thought of changing the title of his own painting. But a poem by Baudelaire, "Invitation to a Journey", made him change his mind. The poem tells of a land where all is "order and beauty/luxury, calm and pleasure". Matisse finished his painting in the autumn.

colour gone wild

When *Luxe, calme et volupté* ("luxury, calm and sensuality") was exhibited in the spring of 1905, Signac bought it at once. Did he realise that this work marked the birth of a new school, which would soon overtake the Neo-Impressionists, then in fashion? For although here colour was still held slightly in check, Matisse was to make it truly explode in the future. Other painters, like the young Raoul Dufy, would get carried along in this whirlwind of colour, which was called Fauvism.

◄ *Reclining Nude* (1907). Sculpture in bronze: 35 x 50 x 27.5 cm.

The idea for this sculpture originated in *Luxe, calme et volupté*. It would often recur in Matisse's work.

Decorative Figure on an Ornamental Background (winter 1925-26), Nice. Oil on canvas: 130 x 98 cm.

Matisse was as interested in the decorative elements as in his model. ►

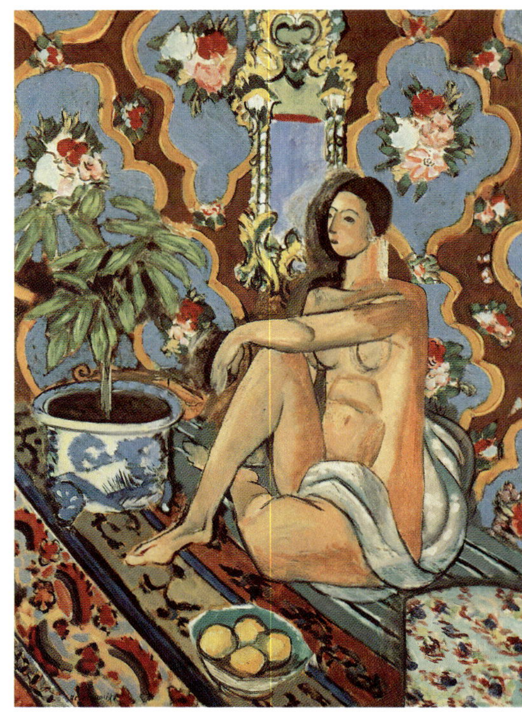

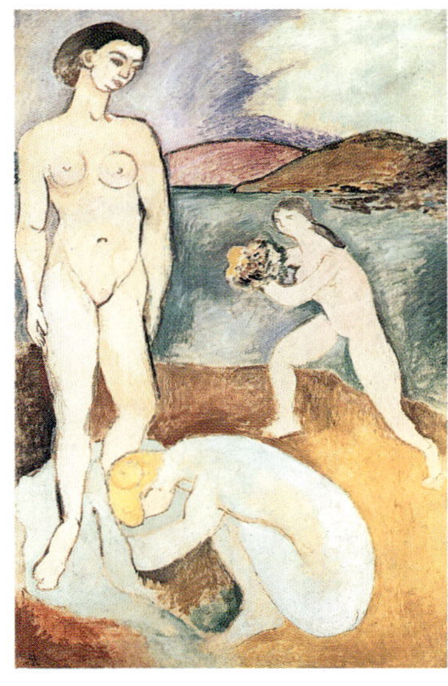

▲
Le luxe I (summer 1907), Collioure. Oil on canvas: 210 x 138 cm.

Three years after *Luxe, calme et volupté,* Matisse partially returned to the theme of nudity, which interested him greatly.

Odalisque in Red Trousers (autumn 1921), Nice. Oil on canvas: 65 x 90 cm. ►

This was the first picture to figure officially in a Paris museum, the Musée du Luxembourg.

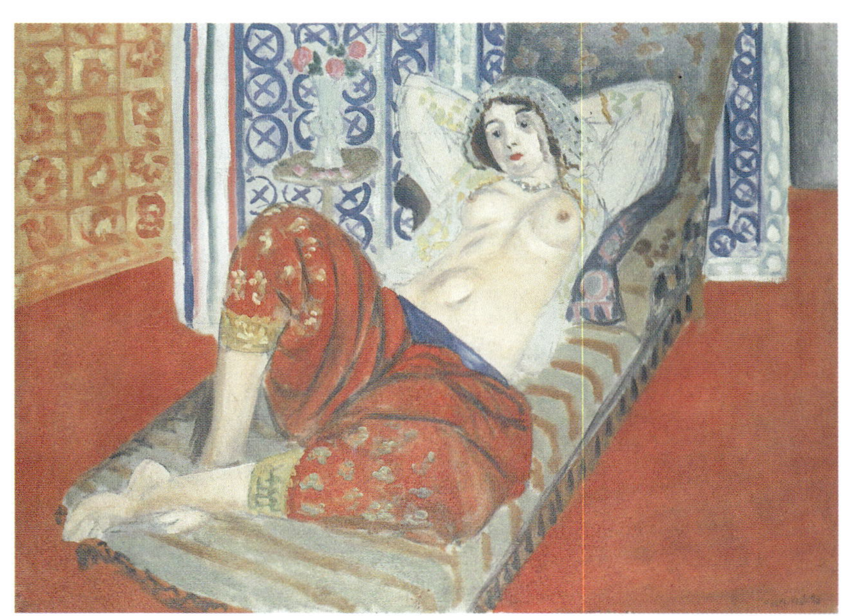

Matisse, or a particular idea of beauty

"What I dream of is an art of balance, purity, calm, without a disturbing subject [...] something like a good armchair".
These very peaceful-sounding words from Matisse, published in 1908 in *La grande revue*, bear no relation to the Fauvist pictures he was then painting. But he felt the need to clear up some misunderstandings. Critics who were offended by his women's faces painted in flamboyant colours had written that he wanted to shock at any price, that he did not care for beauty. Matisse therefore decided to publish his *Notes d'un peintre* ("Notes of a painter") regularly, to explain his work, his ideas and his development. Today these notes are a mine of information.

At the exact moment when Fauvism was triumphing with *Luxe, calme et volupté*, Matisse was seized with doubt. He passionately loved bright colours – yet he could not abandon lines. The underlying drawing was always there in his Pointillist picture, but it was hidden by the paint. How could he reconcile these two modes of expression, line and colour?
It was quite simple: he continued using lines, but drew them with paint so that they were included in the composition. This is perfectly illustrated in *Le luxe I*. He "renders the arabesque directly in colour". That was the answer for those who said that a painter had to choose between colour and line. Matisse himself could have written Baudelaire's words: "The line of the arabesque is the most spiritual of all". "It is like a sign conveying everything all together, which makes one sentence of all sentences", Matisse added.

The Dream (May 1935), Nice. Oil on canvas: 81 x 65 cm.

Lydia Delektorskaya, "the woman with blue eyes", is deep in her dreams. Matisse conveys a gentle stillness through the harmony of pink and blue and a subtle interplay of curved lines. ►

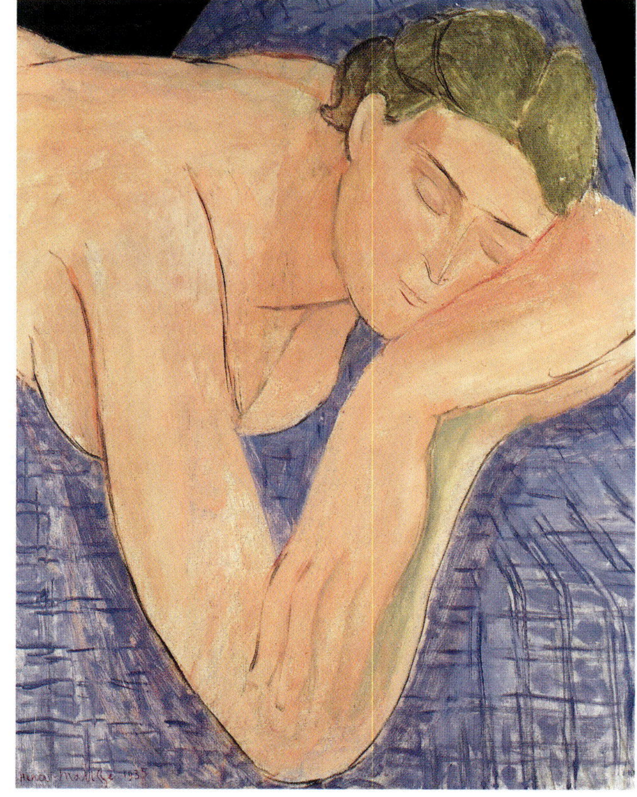

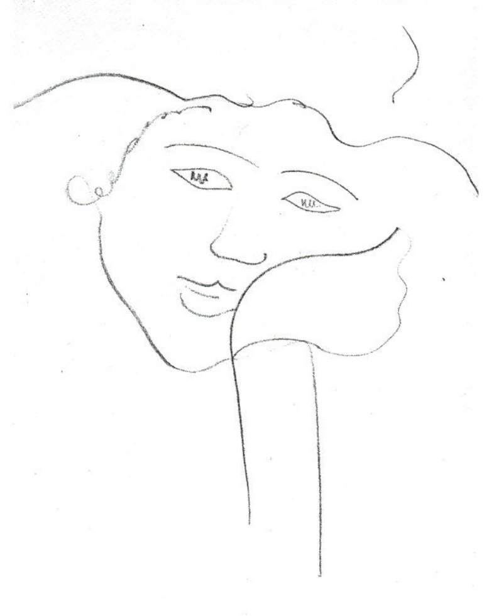

▲
Portrait of Greta Prozor (1916).
Lead pencil on paper: 56 x 37.3 cm.

This is an extraordinary drawing, part of a series of studies for a painted portrait. In a few pencil lines Matisse manages to suggest the personality of the young actress posing for him.

Untitled, *Nude lying on an African Rug* (1935). ►
Pen and black ink on paper: 37.8 x 50.3 cm.

For Matisse "drawing is painting with reduced means". It allowed him to express his emotions just as much as by painting.

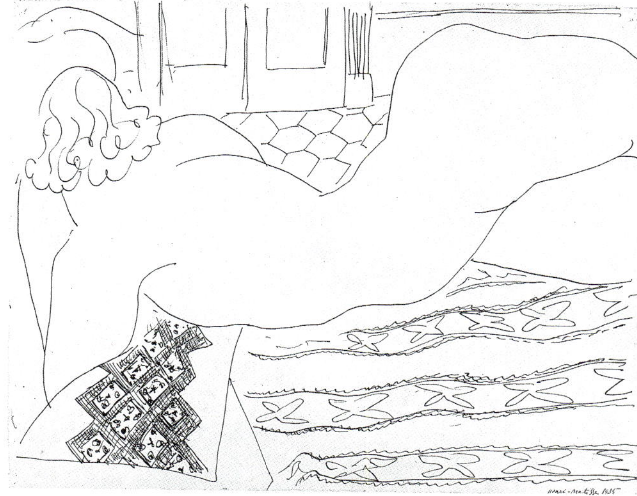

The word "arabesque", meaning a kind of ideal curve, comes from the Italian term *arabesco* and is used for painted or carved decoration characteristic of Islamic art. In Islamic art the arabesque is associated with objects and ideas, since artists are not allowed to represent human beings. But Matisse used it in his own particular way, linking it to feminine beauty. He discovered Islamic art through an enthusiast, the painter Gustave Moreau, whose studio he attended. In 1912 Matisse went twice to Tangiers in Morocco to experience this different culture. Other people would have returned with exotic paintings; Matisse came home with empty hands – it was all in his head. Many years later his memories resurfaced.

In the 1920s Matisse set up a Middle Eastern corner in his studio. He painted the classic theme of the odalisque (from the Arabic word *oda*, meaning "bedroom"). He was not looking for the picturesque, as many of his predecessors were. It was just that this subject allowed him to use naked models who were naked for a reason. This was his way of getting away from the academic nude, who was there simply to be painted. The odalisque also allowed him to introduce decorative elements – fabrics, curtains, carpets, flowers and jewellery – and to convey three-dimensional shapes.
How can a human face be brought to life in the two-dimensional space of a picture? We know that Matisse did not like linear perspective, the illusion that makes us see depth in an image. He was looking for something else: a "perspective of feeling", which he could not obtain with lines and a vanishing point. "To seek out what the line wants, the point where it wants to come in or die" – that was his aim.
There are no ready-made recipes for this. Each time he had to arrange his composition, relying on colour, contours and the arabesque to create a harmony between form and content. To those who criticise the sometimes rather approximate anatomy of his portraits, Matisse replied, not without humour, "If I met anyone like them in the street I would run away in terror. I'm not primarily creating a woman, I'm making a picture."

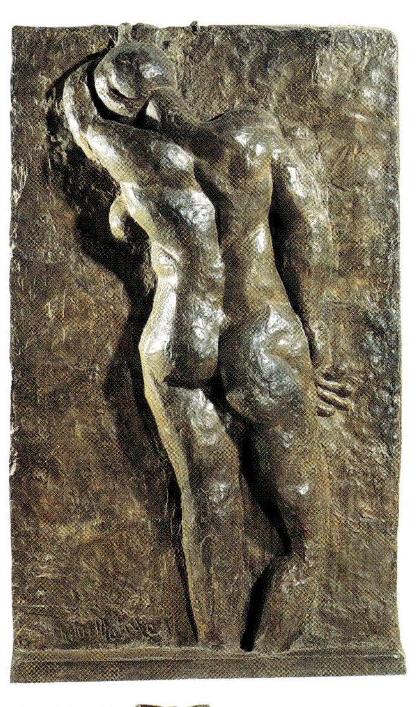
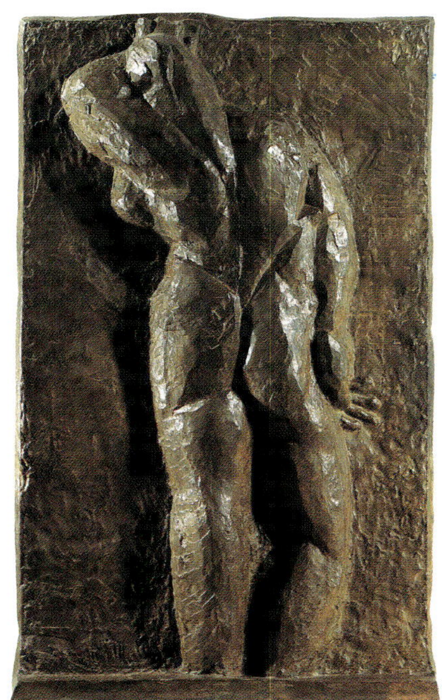
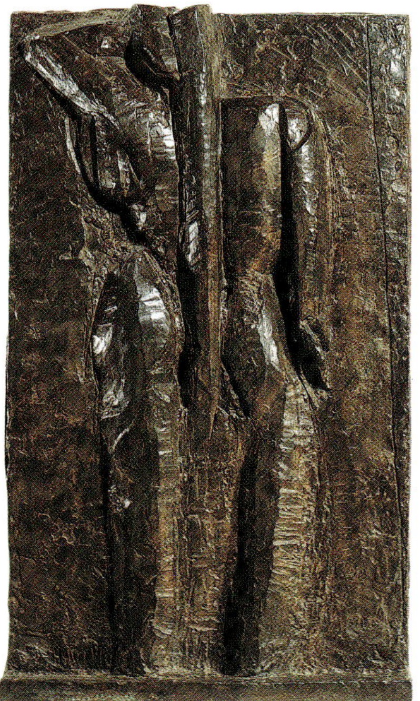
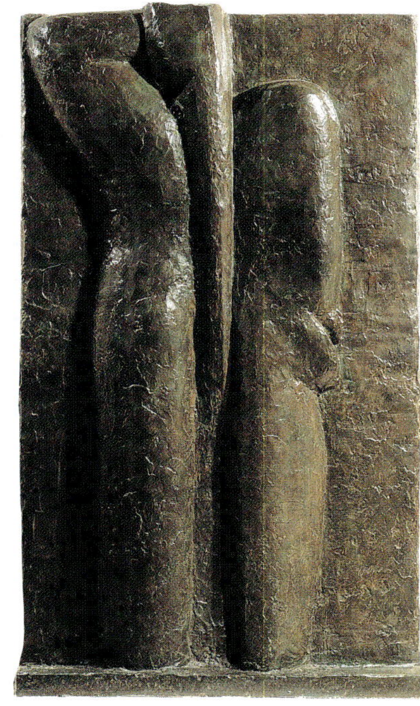

THE BACK

1909 – 1913 – 1916 – 1930

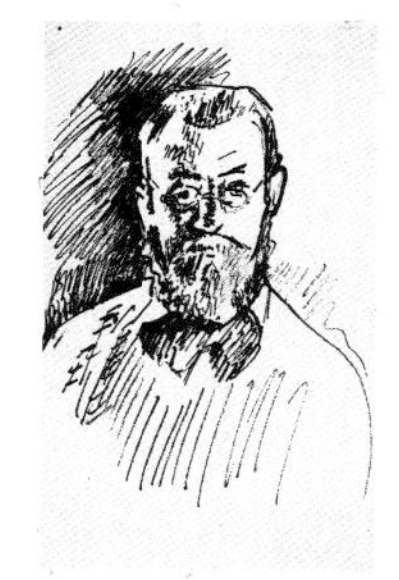

▲ *Self-portrait* (1903). Brush and ink: 34 x 22 cm. Private collection.

From about 1909 Matisse started work on vast sculptures representing a woman who posed for him. He started from scratch three times. But increasingly he forgot about his model to concentrate solely on the three-dimensional shapes.

Matisse loved painting and sculpting women. For five years he had been studying their clothes and their bodies. But he began to dream of something else – still a woman, but the sculpture of a woman, huge, naked and seen from the back.

◀ *The Back I*
Bas-relief (1909).
Bronze:
190 x 116 x 13 cm.
1/10. Cast by Valsuani.

The Back II
Bas-relief (1913).
Bronze:
188 x 116 x 14 cm.
3/10. Cast by Georges Rudier.

The Back III
Bas-relief (1916-17).
Bronze:
190 x 114 x 16 cm.
7/10. Cast by Georges Rudier.

The Back IV
Bas-relief (1930).
Bronze:
190 x 114 x 16 cm.
2/10. Cast by Georges Rudier.

nothing but the back

He decided to make it a bas-relief so that he could sculpt only one visible side: the back. After an initial version in clay, he moved on to plaster. So appeared the earliest known *Back – Back I*.

This relief radiates an incredible feeling of power and strength, as though the sculpted woman were trying to pass through the block of bronze. Matisse treats her with realism; the left leg and arm bear all the weight of the body, while on the right, the arm, buttock and knee are relaxed. At the bottom of the relief the model's feet are cut off by a horizontal bar. Perhaps this is water ...

In 1913, 1916 and 1930 Matisse returned to this work and pursued it. He felt a need to go beyond appearance, beyond the model's image. What interested him was not the woman, but the volume her body occupied in space.

Short history of a sculpture
Before being cast in bronze, these sculptures were made in plaster. The plaster versions have been preserved in the Musée Matisse in Le Cateau-Cambrésis.
For each work he does the sculptor decides how many bronzes should be cast – in this case, ten. This figure appears next to the caster's mark and the artist's signature.

sculpting to be a better painter?

Matisse was both a painter and sculptor, like Daumier or Degas in the 19th century, or Derain and Picasso in the 20th. Degas made wax sculptures of dancers or horses to see more clearly how they occupied space in three dimensions. Picasso, the revolutionary, preferred putting together objects found on rubbish tips.

Matisse followed a more classical style. While he seldom carved stone, he loved to work with clay, plaster or wood, so warm and soft to the touch. His sculptures can usually be held in the hand, since "a sculpture," he said, "should invite us to handle it as an object". Sometimes this helped him to a better understanding of his subject, when, as he said himself, he was tired of painting. But he always remained a painter who sculpted simply to organise his ideas.

▲ Matisse working on the plaster bas-relief (*The Back III*) at Issy-les-Moulineaux. Photograph taken in 1915. Musée Matisse collection, Le Cateau-Cambrésis.

After 1909, when he was living in Issy-les-Moulineaux, Matisse liked to spend time alone in his garden working. But he had started sculpting before then. It was between 1900 and 1909 that he did most of his sculptures, almost 70 pieces.

Serpentine ▶ (1909). Bronze: 56.5 x 29.2 x 19 cm. Musée Matisse, Nice.

For this sculpture Matisse drew on the photograph of a rather plump woman. He slimmed down her shape and, through the curve of her body as it relates to the vertical pillar, gave her a supple movement that is reflected in her name: the "Serpentine" is a dance.

snaking movements

This little *Serpentine* breaks all the rules of anatomy. Some have complained that it's just a caricature of a woman. Certainly Matisse has not created a woman. Instead, though the body is still, he has created movement and rhythm through its lovely arabesque.

With the four heavy versions of *The Back,* Matisse changed his style. He very much admired Cézanne's *Three*

What is a bronze?
Bronze is an alloy of copper and tin that cannot be carved directly. A model must first be made in clay, plaster, wood or marble and a mould of it made. At the foundry a "refractory core", identical to the original, is made. This core is then ground down to reduce its volume, and wax is poured into the gap left between the refractory core and the mould, which is then removed. The sculptor can now rework the wax version. A casting mould is then made around this wax model using fire clay, and the whole is heated to melt the wax, which runs out through a network of pipes. The mould is then surrounded with a cap, heated to 600° C and the molten bronze, at a temperature of 1200° C, is poured down the pipes. Finally, the mould is broken and the bronze sculpture emerges.

Bathers and drew inspiration from the seated woman on the right of this painting, seen from the back, to sculpt his bas-relief. He was trying to integrate his figures into space, as Cézanne does. He also wanted his sculpted figure to melt into the plaster block.

when form disappears

In 1913 Matisse made a second, broader *Back*. The woman is leaning more heavily on her left leg, but the shapes are simplified. Her head and neck form a single mass, like the bather's hair. What did Matisse want? To retain the essentials, to find the lines of force, to simplify through distortion. In 1913 he had not yet reached the end of his path.
At this moment he had no idea that it would take another 17 years to achieve his aim.

Look at a painting by Cézanne. Everything in it is so well integrated that from any distance and however many figures there are, you can clearly see the bodies and understand which limb belongs to which figure. Matisse, *Notes d'un peintre* (1908).

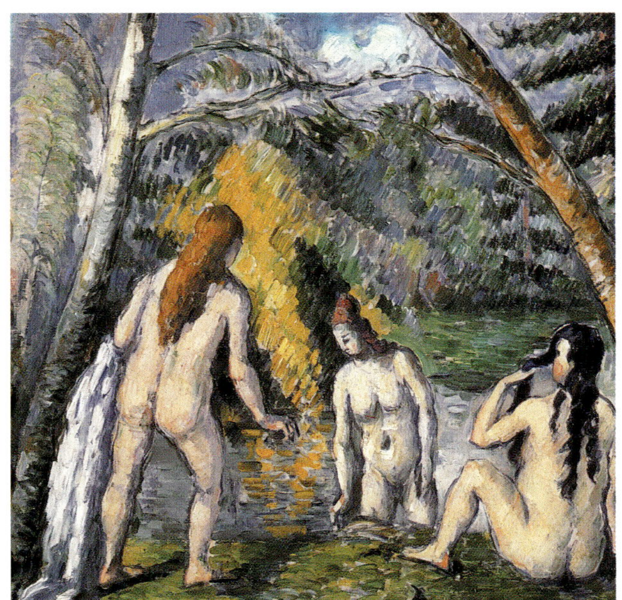

◀ **Paul Cézanne,** *Three Bathers* (1879-82). Oil on canvas: 60.6 x 54.6 cm, Musée du Petit Palais, Paris.

Matisse bought this picture in 1899 from the art dealer Ambroise Vollard. Thirty-seven years later he gave it to the Musée du Petit Palais, not wishing to keep the masterpiece to himself. Many titles of his paintings include the word "bathers".

in search of harmony

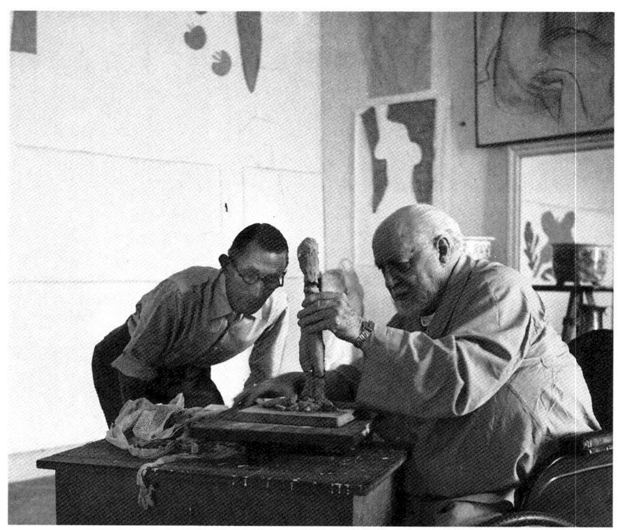

◄ Matisse with the bronze caster Valsuani at the Hôtel Régina. Photograph taken in Nice after 1938.

To produce a bronze sculpture, sculptor and caster must work together. In 1909 Matisse first approached Valsuani, who made the first in the series *The Back*.

Why should a back not be as expressive as a face? From 1892 and his first painted study for *The Back,* Matisse was so sure that it could that he always refused to paint the face when his model was turned towards him. To hell with the likeness that paralyses imagination! “Expression does not lie in the passion that fills a

Aristide Maillol (1861-1944), *Desire* (1908). Bas-relief in lead: 120 x 115 x 25 cm. Musée d'Orsay, Paris. ►

The sculptor Maillol made very different bas-reliefs from those of Matisse. His work is more like ancient sculpture, whereas Matisse's is in the tradition of Michelangelo and the Renaissance.

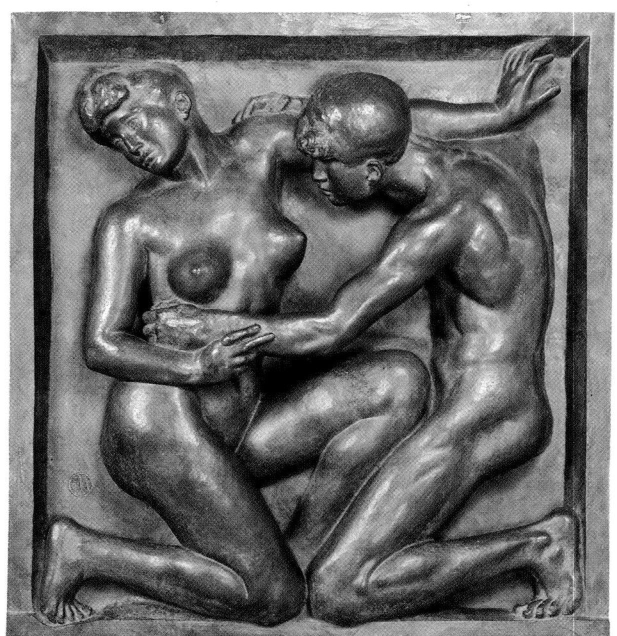

What is a relief?
Unlike a shape the sculptor can walk around, a relief is sculpted on a flat surface. The sculptor can set the figures into the background: this is a bas-relief or low relief. Or they can be entirely detached from the background or partially detached, with only a few points of contact: this is called high relief.

Did Matisse know Rodin?
Matisse met Rodin at the Hôtel Biron, where both were living and working. This 18th-century hotel, a former palace, had belonged to the Church and in 1908 became a community of artists. Writers Jean Cocteau and Rainer Maria Rilke, the dancer Isadora Duncan, the Romanian actor De Max, and Jeanne Bloch, a cabaret singer, all lived there. In 1910 the state bought the hotel and evicted its tenants. After a petition had been organised, it became the Musée Rodin in 1916.

face," he said. "It is in the entire arrangement of my picture; the place the figures occupy, the spaces around them, the proportions, all play a part."
The sculptor Rodin shared this view. He refused to be a slave to anatomy and preferred to look at how life shaped a figure. He reflected the interior – the feeling – through the exterior, such as a taut muscle.

a nude... a wall

But Matisse went further. He did not want to create the illusion of a real body by smoothing his sculpture to differentiate the smoothness of skin from the roughness of the material; he was particularly concerned not to separate his figure from the material.
The third *Back* is formed simply of large blocks that melt into the wall. The body's weight is now balanced on both legs, and the hair and spine form a single mass.
Matisse reached the harmony he was searching for with *The Back IV*. The body has finally found its axis, around which the different elements are organised. The interplay of hollows and raised surfaces, shadow and light, makes this back radiant. It has a profound beauty which goes beyond appearance. The extraordinary story of *The Back* was finished. Had the back of a figure emerged with such maturity before?

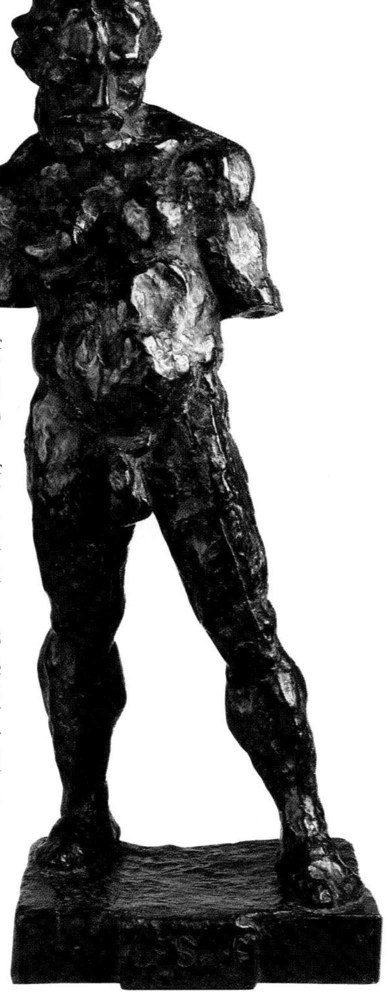

The Slave, (1900-03). ▶
Bronze:
92.3 x 33 x 30.5 cm.
Musée Matisse, Nice.

This sculpture is often compared to Rodin's *Walking Man* (1878). Both sculptors used the same model, Bevilacqua-Pignatelli.

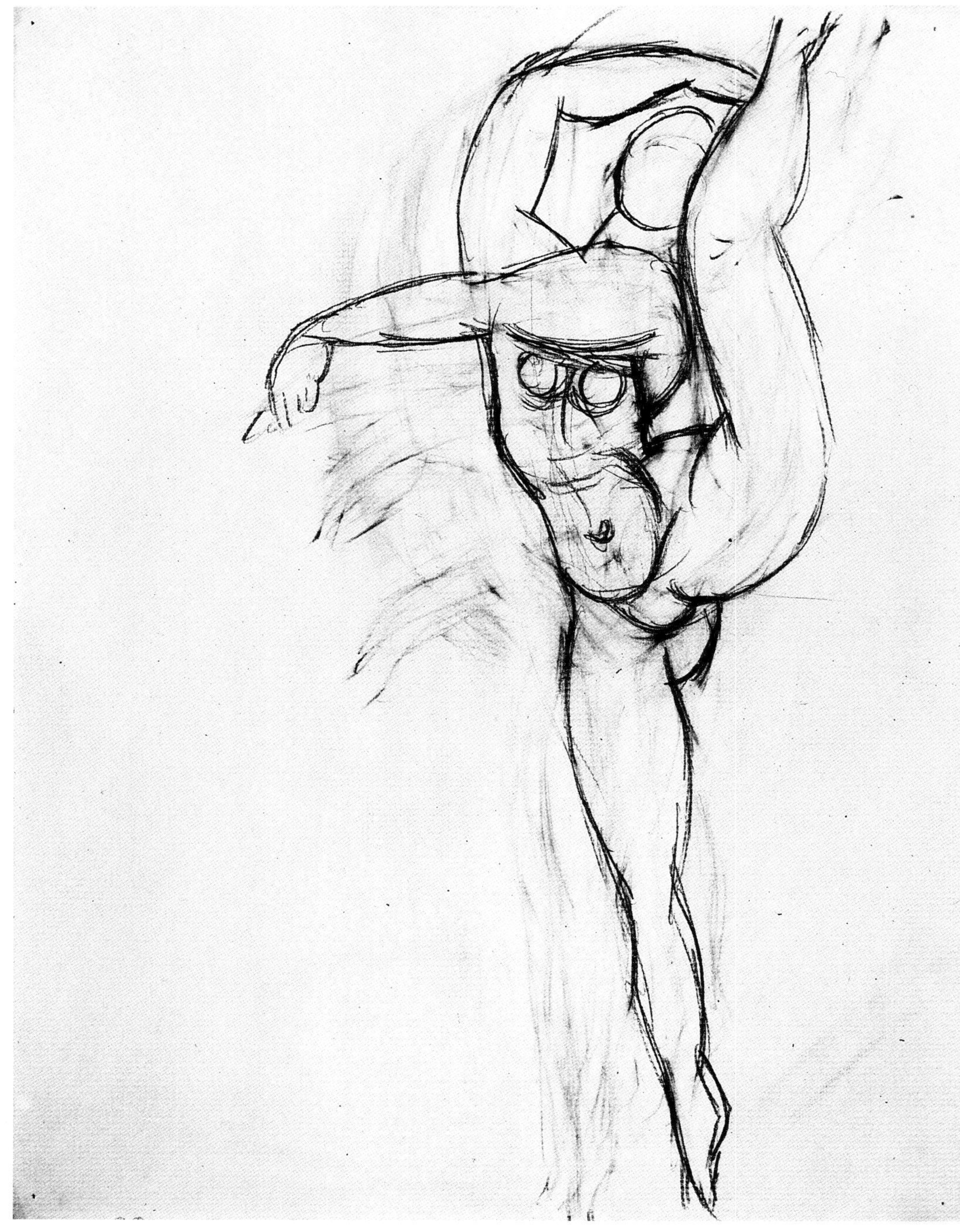

THE DANCER

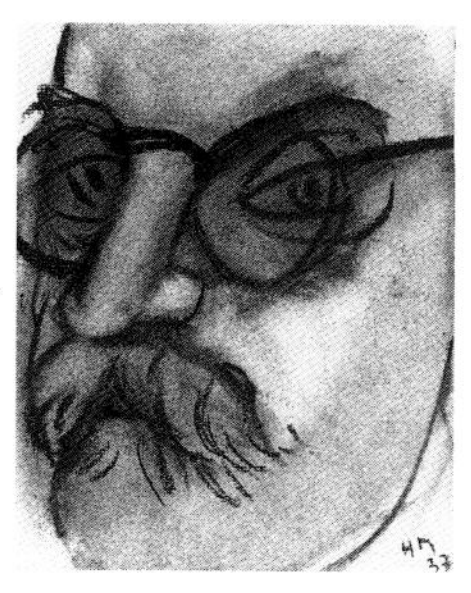

▲ *Self-portrait* (1937). Charcoal on paper, mounted on blank paper: 25.4 x 20.3 cm.

This preliminary drawing was the beginning of a great adventure: aged 60, Matisse discovered America.

New York, Chicago, Los Angeles, San Francisco, Philadelphia: Matisse made two trips to America in the same year, 1930. The first was to see the country, the second to sit on the judges' panel for a painting competition. There he met his friend Dr Barnes, who asked him to decorate a huge wall above the three French windows of the drawing-room in his villa at Merion, Pennsylvania.

balance and pirouette

A picture without a drawing is like a house without a frame. Matisse.

Matisse was delighted. He returned to Paris and started on a series of small sketches. Early in 1931, after returning to Merion, he set to work. He made hundreds of sketches, all of the same subject: dance. This dancer, caught in movement, was one of them. Matisse captures the body's shapes in a few lines: two round balls for the breasts, a few curves for the muscles. Once again, he forgets about the face. What interests him is movement. So he outlines the large shapes, then rubs them out and starts again. To convey both balance and pirouette, he defines a central axis around which the rest of the body turns and the movement takes shape. It is as though the woman of *The Back IV* had overcome her weight and was spinning at last!

◀ *Dancer* (1930-31). Graphite pencil on paper: 32.2 cm high, 25.7 cm wide.

why choose dance?

It was settled: Matisse, painter of the joy of living, as he was known, was inviting Dr Barnes to accept a dance. What could be more magnificent and more alive than dance! Particularly dancing in a circle. Matisse loved to paint the movement of dancers and, after 30 years, this was no new experiment.

join the dance

His first painting of dancers in a ring dates from 1905. The painting called *The Joy of Living* showed nude figures in the background, dancing a farandole.

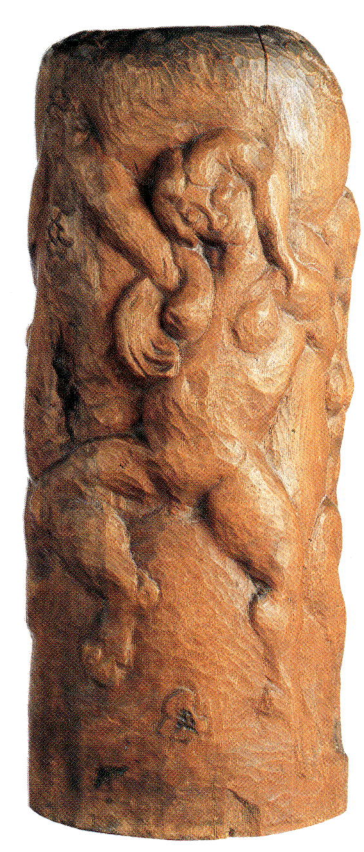

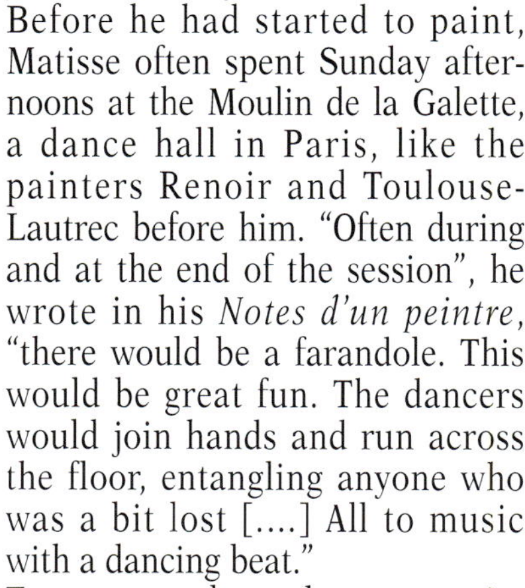

Before he had started to paint, Matisse often spent Sunday afternoons at the Moulin de la Galette, a dance hall in Paris, like the painters Renoir and Toulouse-Lautrec before him. "Often during and at the end of the session", he wrote in his *Notes d'un peintre*, "there would be a farandole. This would be great fun. The dancers would join hands and run across the floor, entangling anyone who was a bit lost [....] All to music with a dancing beat."

Twenty years later, these memories surfaced. The idea of painting a dance at Merion was not really linked to the space he was given. Like music, dance was part of Matisse: "The whole composition, all the dancers are together dancing to the same rhythm'.

Early in 1931 Matisse began looking for a studio large enough to hold the 72 square metres of canvas

What was he looking for in America?
When Matisse went to America and Tahiti in 1930 it was not for escape or rest. He was looking for new spaces and different light. Yet, though he was stunned by the beauty of Tahiti, Matisse felt crushed by the sun, "As though the light had stopped moving forever. As though life was fixed in a magnificent pose." It was in New York, which he called "the golden nugget", that he found the feeling of freedom and space he was looking for.

◄ *Dance* (1907). Bas-relief in wood: 43.2 x 15.2 cm. Musée Matisse, Nice.

This little round sculpture in wood enabled Matisse to shape a body in continuous movement.

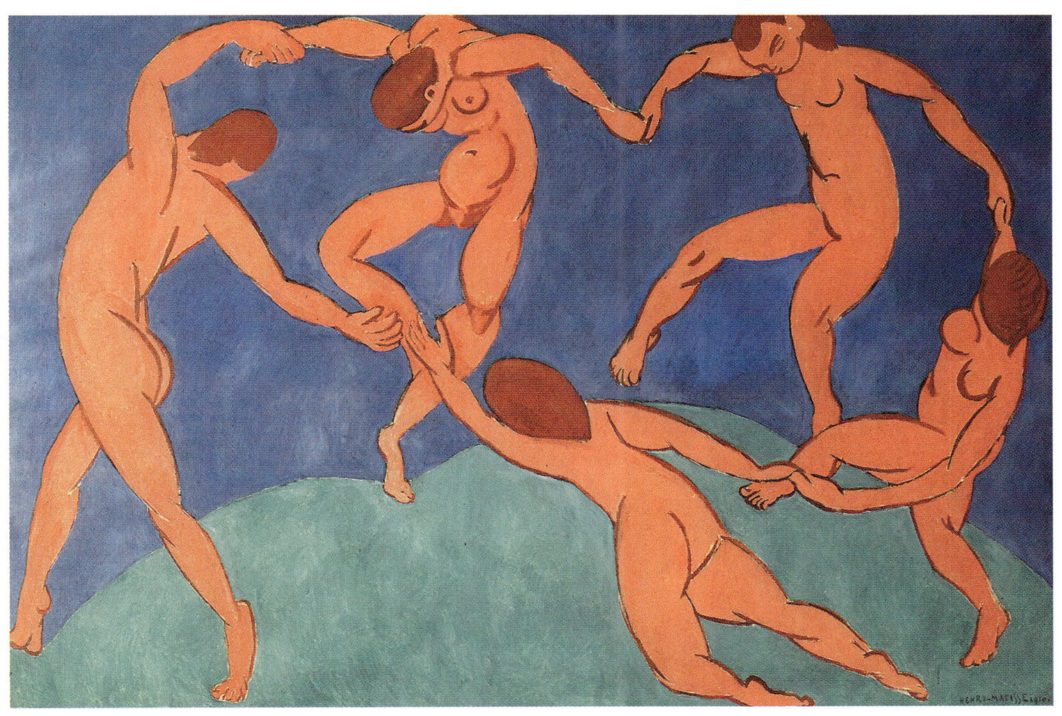

▲
Dance (1909-10).
Oil on canvas:
260 x 391 cm.
Hermitage Museum,
St Petersburg.

Everything has been reduced to its essential lines and to three colours: "the azure of the sky, the pink of the bodies, the green of the hill".

Shchukin's commission
In 1909 a great Russian merchant-collector Sergey Shchukin commissioned Matisse to decorate his private residence, the former palace of the Trubetskoy princes in Moscow. Matisse designed three large panels, one for each floor, but only two were completed, *Dance* and *Music*.

that would cover the wall in Merion. He finally found a disused cinema at 8 Rue Desiré Niel and set to work.

staging the dance

The painting was done on three panels shaped like rounded arches joined together lower down. Matisse had to compose his picture according to its surroundings, as though the canvas extended into the room and garden.
There could not have been a better place for him to paint this gigantic enterprise.

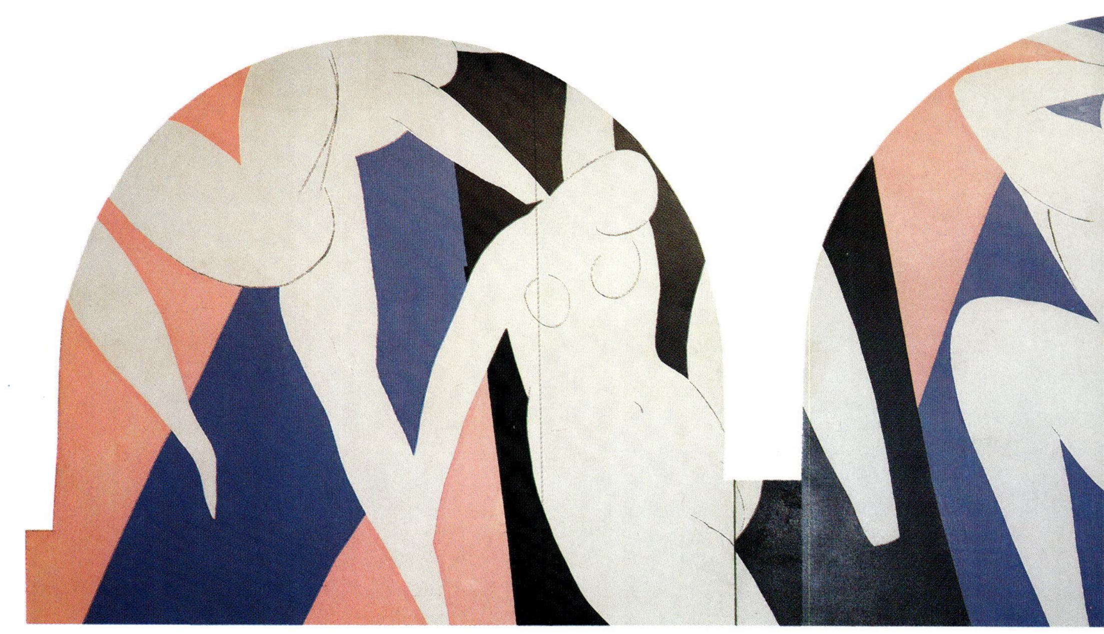

how to bring in colour?

After hundreds of sketches and 30 or so preliminary versions of the entire painting, Matisse conveyed his complete design to the canvas. As this could not be done using grids of corresponding squares, he had to do something else. He tied a piece of charcoal to the end of a cane and drew his eight dancers directly.

The next problem was to test the colours. To avoid making mistakes and spoiling his design, Matisse painted in gouache on paper, which he cut up and pinned to his canvas. This allowed him to modify his colours as he chose. The first version, which was not discovered until 1992, had only two colours, grey for the bodies and blue for the background. The second version has four, grey, blue, black and pink.

In spring 1932 the canvas was ready. But it was a disaster; Matisse had got the wrong measurements for the

Corresponding squares
When an artist is painting a large picture, he starts by doing a smaller sketch. To enlarge it, he divides it into squares. He then draws a grid with the same number of squares of whatever size he wants on the final surface and reproduces the sketch, square by square.

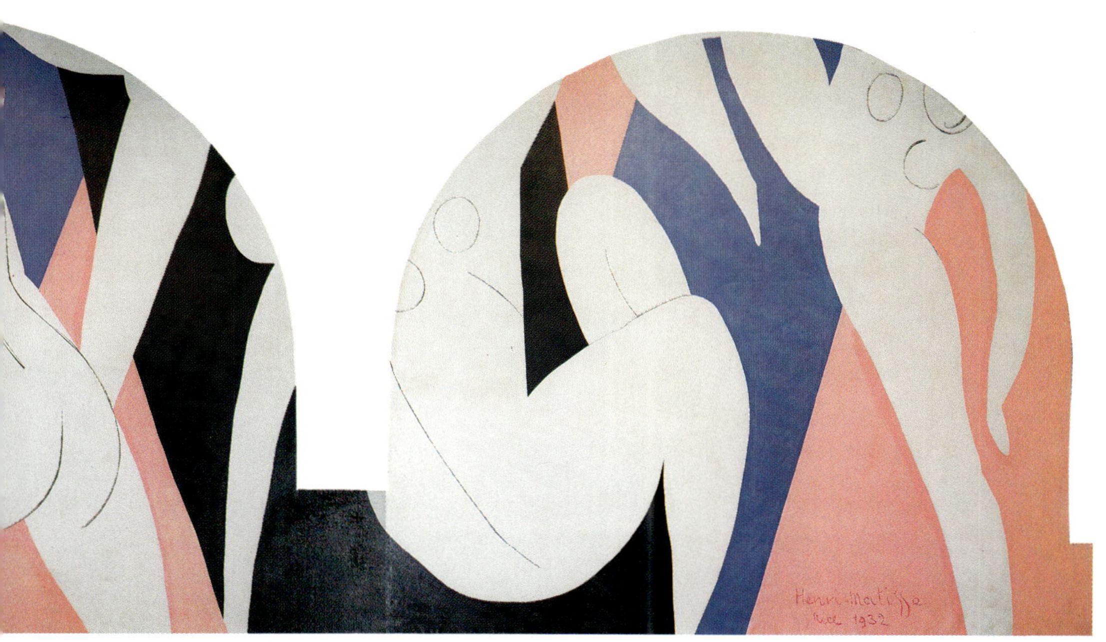

▲
The Dance (1931-32). Oil on canvas: 333 x 391 cm. Musée d'Art Moderne de la Ville de Paris, Paris.

This painting is not, as is sometimes thought, the first version of *The Dance* commissioned by Barnes, but the second. Matisse had to do a third: the measurements for the room were wrong!

wall. Its pendentives were twice as big as he had thought. What could be done? Change the panel? Make a replica of a different size? Impossible. This painting had been designed as an integral part of the space. Because it was to decorate a wall, Matisse had used single hues that looked as though they had been plastered on. Because he was using flat blocks of colour, he used line and contrast to suggest three-dimensional shapes. Despite limited space, he had succeeded in giving an impression of freedom, as though the figures were entering and leaving the painted space. One small modification would have completely destroyed the harmony. So he had to start all over again. A year later, Matisse finished the third and final version. Dr Barnes was filled with admiration, exclaiming that it was "like the rose window of a cathedral!"

stage design

◀ *The Emperor's Dancers* (1920). Ink on paper, sketch for *Le rossignol* ("The song of the nightingale"). Fonds Kochno, Bibliothèque de l'Opéra, Paris.

Theatre set design was an important experience for Matisse, since it meant envisaging the movement of colours or, as here, arranging characters on stage.

Painting *The Dance* for the house at Merion was a fascinating experience for Matisse. Yet this was not his first attempt at this kind of work. Ten years earlier in 1919, he had received a visit from the Director of the Ballets Russes, Sergey Diaghilev, and the composer Igor Stravinsky. The two men asked Matisse to design the set, curtains, costumes and props for Stravinsky's ballet *Le rossignol* ("The song of the nightingale"). The contract was signed in September.
Matisse's main problem was to create a set that would fit into the space of the stage; it had to be sufficiently expressive not to lose its power in the presence of the

The pointed arch
The pointed arch consists of two concave curved lines that meet in a point under a vault. It is the characteristic shape of vaults and windows in Gothic churches. It contrasts with the rounded form of the Romanesque arch.

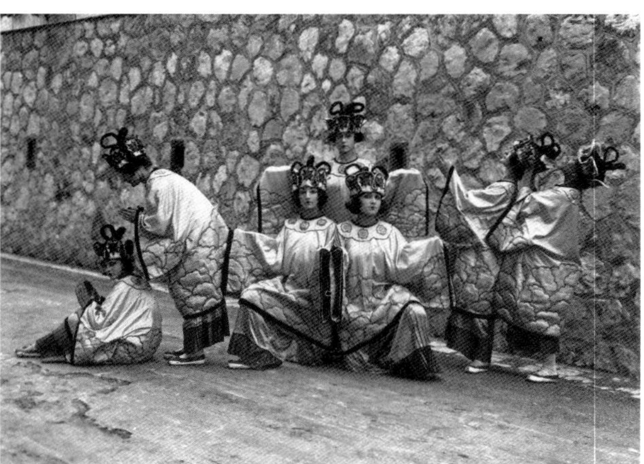

◀ The Monte Carlo set as designed by Matisse, photographed in 1920. Fonds Kochno, Bibliothèque de l'Opéra, Paris.

The emperor's dancers, dressed in costumes designed by Matisse, are gathered in the street. The choreographer, Massine, followed the painter's instructions to the letter.

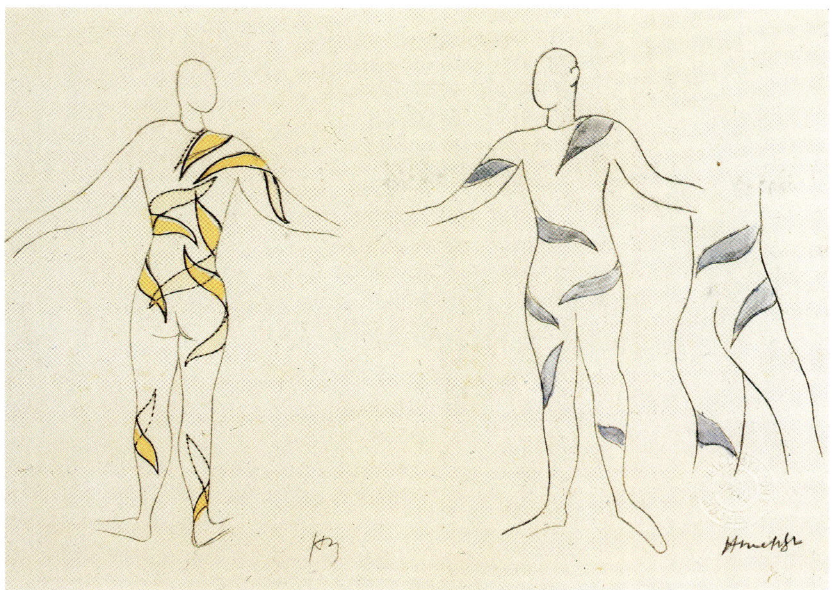

◄ Study for a costume for *The strange farandole* (1938). Fonds Kochno, Bibliothèque de l'Opéra, Paris.

Matisse returned to theatre design in 1938, with *The strange farandole*, a Russian ballet to music by Shostakovich, choreographed by Massine.

Painters and the Ballets Russes
Sergey Diaghilev, director and creator of the Russian Ballet troupe, staged a number of avant-garde works, whose choreography and music frequently caused a scandal. Diaghilev was also good at choosing painters for the sets and costumes. Besides Matisse, there was Picasso, who designed for them more frequently (*Parade*, 1917, *The Three-cornered Hat*, 1919, *Pulcinella*, 1920, *Quadro flamenco*, 1921, *Train bleu*, 1924). But Diaghilev also commissioned work from Robert and Sonia Delaunay, André Derain, De Chirico, Max Ernst and Juan Gris.

dancers. He made a model out of a box, which he lit with an electric light. Inside he arranged the characters as pieces of coloured paper. This was the origin of the gouache paper cut-outs that he used to paint *The Dance* for Merion.

caught up in the dance

In 1937 Matisse was again drawn to the Russian Ballet. He designed the sets and costumes for *The strange farandole*, danced to Shostakovich's Second Symphony. The influence of *The Dance*, finished four years earlier, is clear: a similar setting, with pointed arches, the same simple forms and colours, with dancers dressed in white, yellow, blue, black and red. Produced at Monte Carlo in 1938, the ballet came to Paris in June 1939 and New York in 1940-41 entitled *Red and Black*.
After *The Dance* designed for Merion, Matisse began in a new genre, that of decorative painting. He never abandoned it. One of his last works, the Chapelle du Rosaire in Vence, was designed just like a stage set.

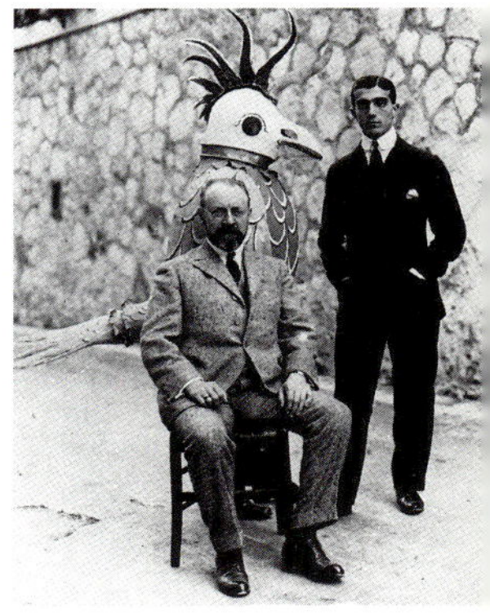

▲
Matisse and Massine at Monte Carlo, photographed in 1920. Fonds Kochno, Bibliothèque de l'Opéra, Paris.

Matisse liked to adopt the roles of his models, as he is ready to do here.

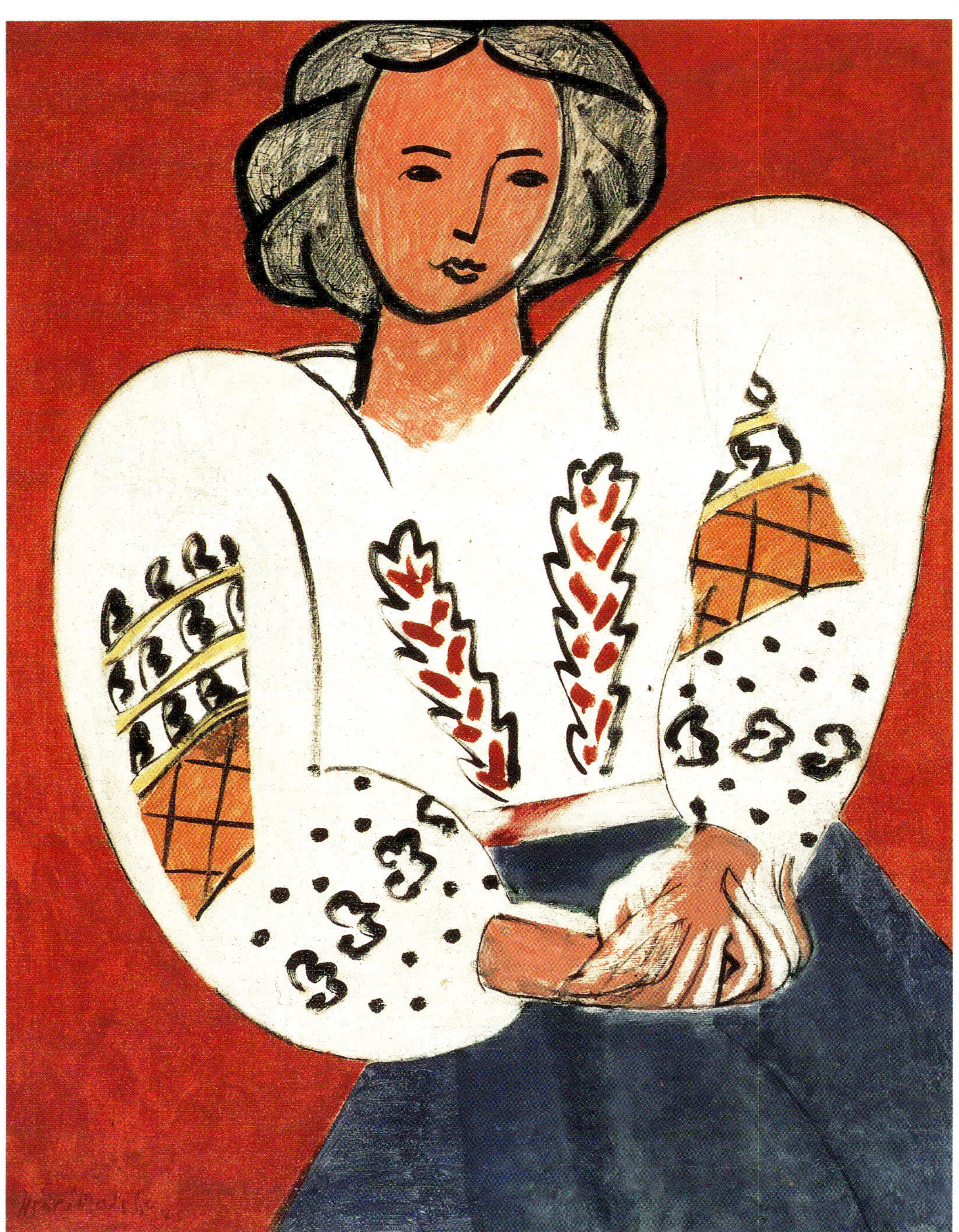

THE ROMANIAN BLOUSE

1940

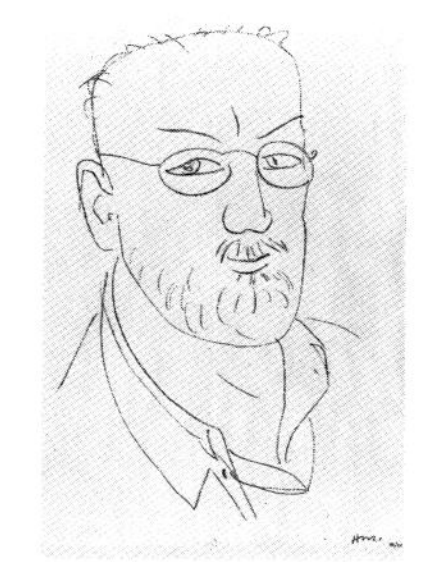

▲ *Self-portrait* (1944). Lithograph: 22.2 x 24 cm. Bibliothèque National, Paris.

Matisse weaves cashmere, tarlatan, muslin, mottling, lace. His pencil is the shuttle and his loom is the weft of a canvas.
André Verdet, *Prestiges de Matisse*, 1952.

Matisse painted this picture in 1940. It took nine months to paint, nine months of simplification, paring down to the essentials.

Three colours invade the space, the vermilion of the background, the ultramarine of the skirt and the totally, unbelievably pure white of the blouse. This white did not come out of a tube; it is the white of the canvas, which Matisse did not paint. Next, the painter added a few touches only, the lemon yellow embroidery, red ochre for the skin, yellow ochre on the sleeves, a few red strokes on the blouse and grey for the hair.

black lines on flat colours

I've worked all these years so that people will say: Matisse is no more than that!
Matisse.

The blue of the skirt is not uniform. Darker bands mark the folds of the cloth. But everywhere else three dimensionality seems to have been effaced. Matisse applied the paint in flat blocks, without varying the tones.
He outlined the shapes with black lines, some thick and opaque – the oval of the face, the neck, the hair and the geometrical patterns on the blouse – others thin and transparent – around the sleeves.
A few black lines separate the fingers from the ochre mass of the hands, and these are lit with strokes of white. With unbroken lines only Matisse suggests the eyes, nose, mouth and hair, without more detail. He has successfully created a painting that is stripped bare, yet amazingly strong.

◄ *The Romanian Blouse* (1940). Oil on canvas: 92 cm high, 73 cm wide.

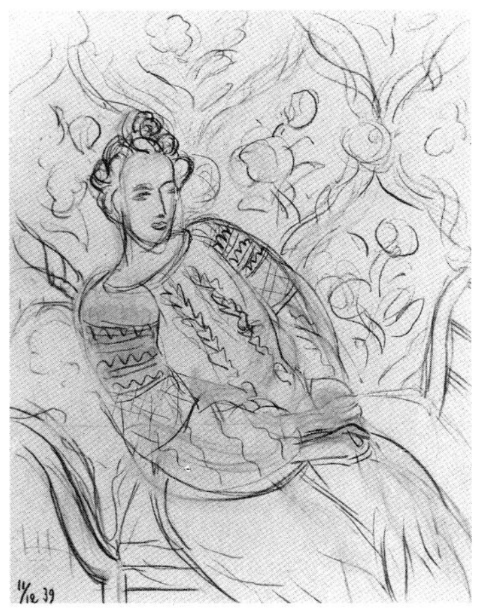

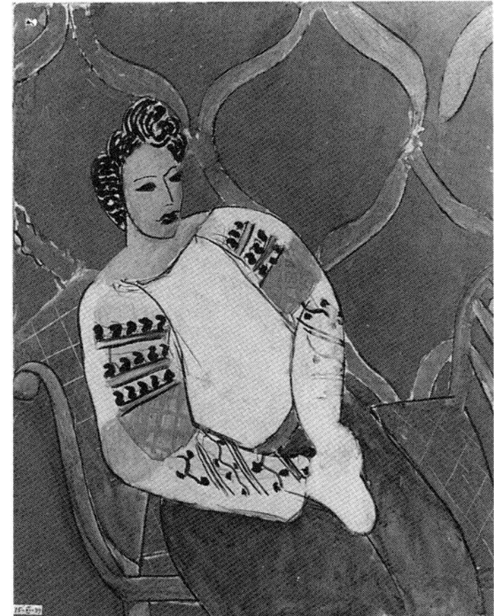

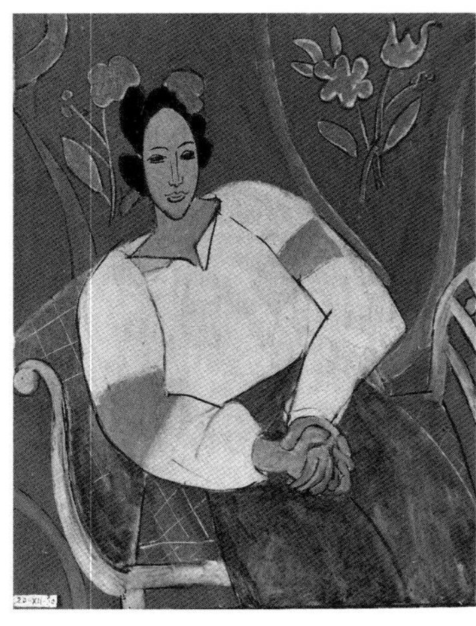

photography works for painters

Before putting a colour on canvas, Matisse would try it out first. He knew that what a red looked like would depend on whether it was next to blue or yellow, so he experimented. He would apply the first colour, the one closest in feeling to what he wanted to express. As soon as he added another, the effect would change. So the line had to be altered. But if he altered the line ...
He knew the theory of colour and the law of contrast. But he trusted his instinct alone, which told him when he had achieved purity, brilliance and harmony.

▲
Here are 6 of the 14 successive stages of *The Romanian Blouse*. Photographs taken by Matisse, signed and dated (stages 1, 3, 5, 9, 12, 14).

fourteen stages for one picture

Matisse made many studies in paint. So as not to waste too many canvases, he would recycle them by scratching off the paint. But in doing so he would remove weeks of work. This did not worry him much: "a painter has only one enemy," he said, "his bad pictures". All the same, in 1935 he began to photograph his studies.

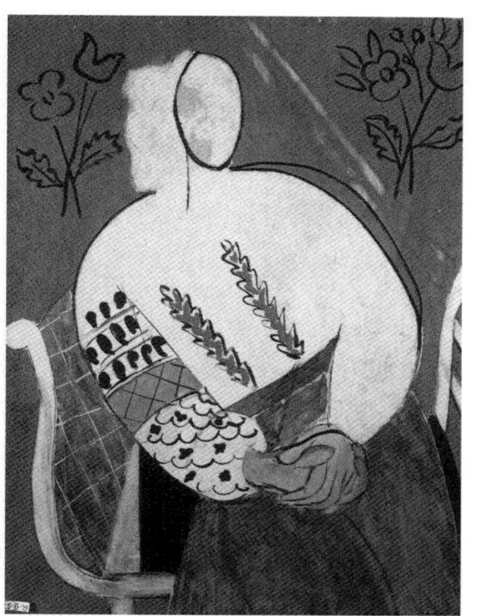

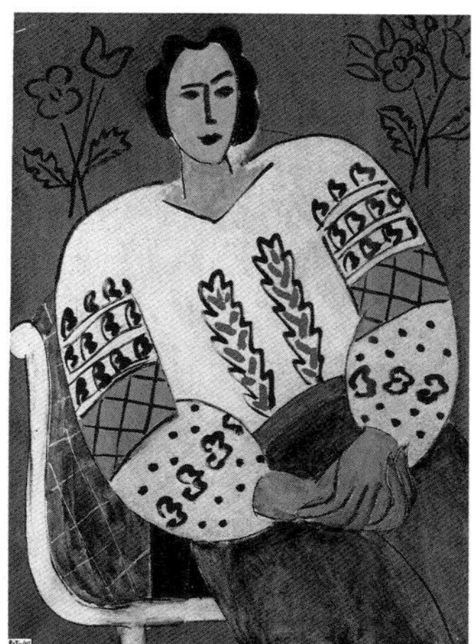

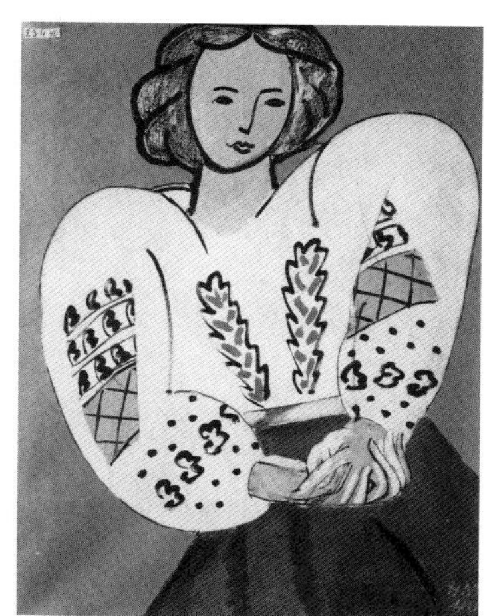

The 14 photographs Matisse took of *The Romanian Blouse* show the development of his work. At first he concentrated on the background, a setting with flowers, and painted the young woman from a rather high angle; he put her in an armchair to locate her in the space.
Gradually he refined his work, brought the model to face forwards, did away with the background and armchair, allowing the sleeves and face to fill the space. The result is all softness and grace.

nothing but the essentials

To art historians, photographs of works in progress are treasures. Those of Picasso's painting *Guernica* show the painter gradually adding more and more elements until the result is a very rich work. Those taken by Matisse show how, on the contrary, that he proceeded by elimination. He gradually removed everything that was superfluous and ended up with only the essentials.

Matisse and Picasso
In the mid-20th century two painters dominated Western art: Matisse from France and Picasso from Spain. They were nicknamed "North Pole" and "South Pole" by Fernande Olivier, Picasso's partner. They met in 1906 at the house of their mutual friends the Steins. Throughout their lives they exchanged paintings, and in 1970-71 Picasso evoked Matisse by using the pattern of *The Romanian Blouse* in his *Old Man Seated* (Musée Picasso, Paris).

why use a model to paint?

This embroidered blouse had fascinated Matisse for years and even if he didn't care about its texture in his painting, he loved the feel of cloth. In 1936 it appeared in numerous drawings.

Often he would give his wife – a milliner – and daughter advice when they were buying clothes. In 1919 he made a magnificent hat with ostrich feathers for his model Antoinette.

"Why use a model?" asked a friend in surprise. "To get further away from her," replied the painter. When Matisse painted a face, he gave it an expression, but not that of the model. In *The Romanian Blouse*, for example, the softness of the face comes partly from the slightly asymmetrical shape of the chin. It also comes from the curved lines, with the ballooning sleeves that invade the space.

Seated Dancer (1939). Charcoal and stump on Montval paper: 65.5 x 50.5 cm.

This drawing was a sketch for a painting (in the Toledo Museum, Ohio) that Matisse finished at the beginning of 1940. The dancer is wearing ◄ the Romanian blouse.

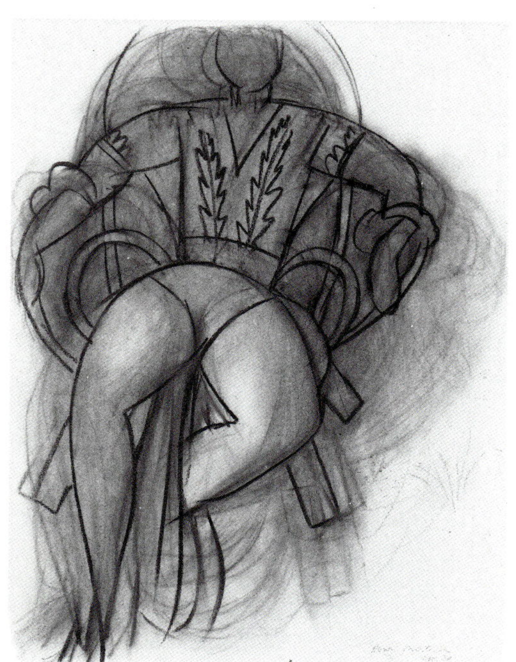

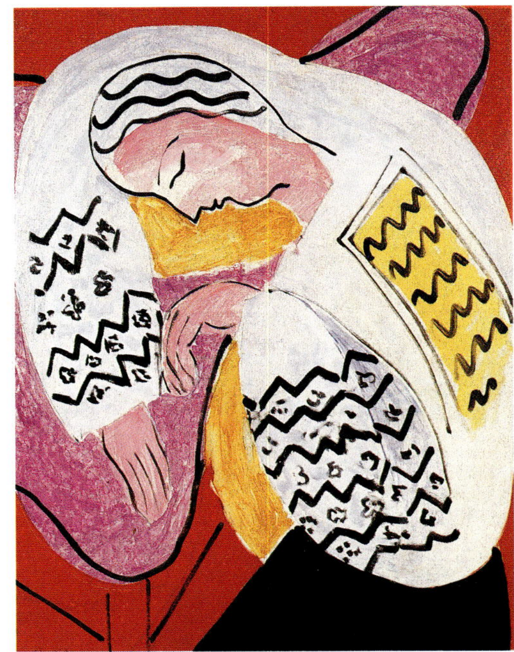

Matisse and the war
None of Matisse's pictures refer to World War II. But his correspondence with his friends Bonnard and Rouveyre and with his son Pierre, then living in New York, reveals his anxiety. Yet he refused to leave France, declined an invitation to go to San Francisco and cancelled his planned trip to Brazil in June 1940. "If everyone of any worth left France, what would be left of France?"
Letter to Pierre Matisse.

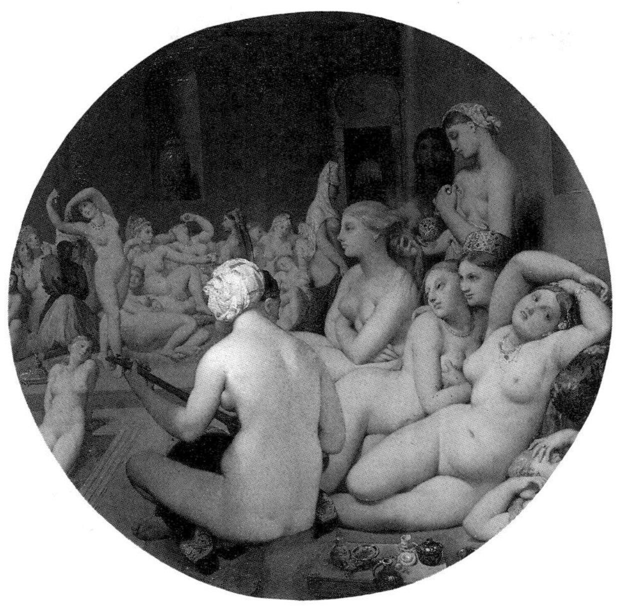

◀ **Jean-Auguste-Dominique Ingres** (1760-1867), *The Turkish Bath* (1862). Oil on canvas: diameter 110 cm. The Louvre, Paris.

"Beautiful forms are flat planes with curves". Ingres' motto describes Matisse's perfectly. He too used the feminine arabesque to celebrate beauty.

The same sort of line appears in *The Dream*, which was also painted during World War II, apparently curled in on itself. But here it speaks of discouragement and abandonment. This is one of the few paintings in which Matisse expressed his anxiety.

gracious feminine curves

These delicate arabesques are reminiscent of Ingres, a 19th-century painter whom Matisse much admired. Ingres was so concerned with the harmony of line that he would give a woman a few extra vertebrae, or round a stiff neck.
There is none of this distortion in Matisse's work. A doctor who collected his work observed from his drawings that Matisse knew anatomy perfectly well. The blouse is not there to hide the woman's body but to set it off.

◀ *The Dream* (1940). Oil on canvas: 81 x 65 cm. Private collection.

This painting was hung in Matisse's apartment as a pendant to both *The Romanian Blouse* and *Male Model*, painted in 1900.

Study for *Window in Nice* (1917-18). Pen and black ink on paper (leaf from a sketchbook): 27.4 x 21.3 cm.

Half-open shutters frequently recur in Matisse's work. They are a point of transition between inside and outside. ►

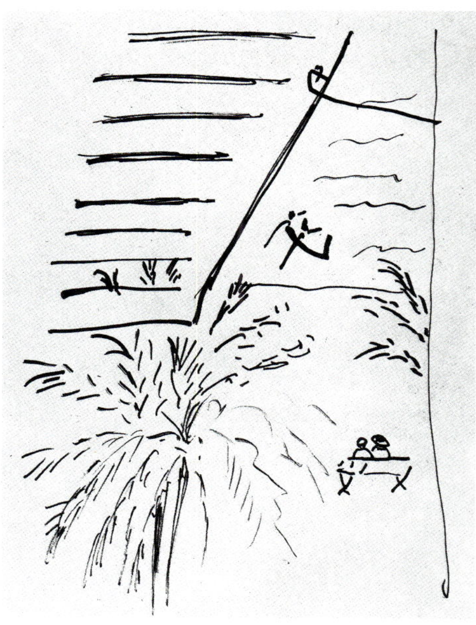

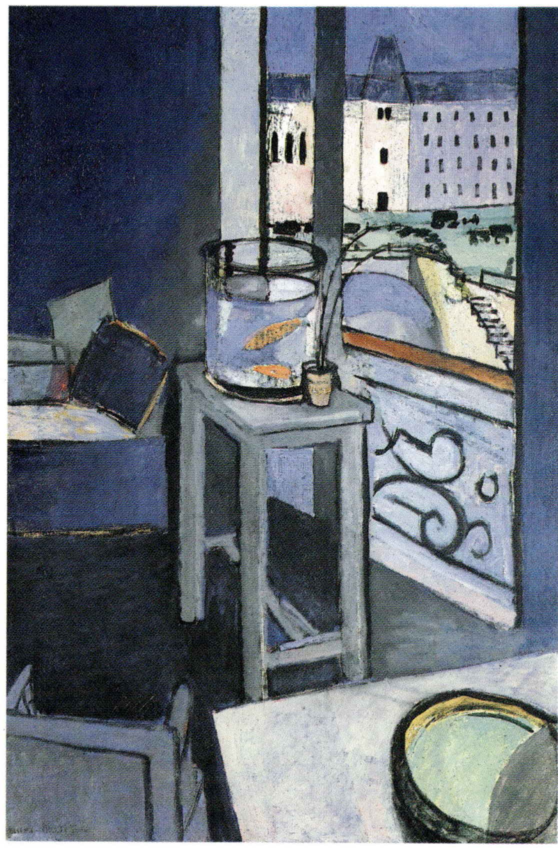

▲
Interior with Goldfish (1914), Paris. Oil on canvas: 147 x 97 cm.

Where does the inside end and the outside begin? The stems of the plant on the table curve towards the steps over on the other side of the river. No water is visible apart from that in the fishbowl, inside.

Interior in Nice, the Siesta (c. 1922), Nice. Oil on canvas: 66 x 54.4 cm.
▼

Hot outside, cool inside. The palm trees are very near, as much present as the flowers in the vase.

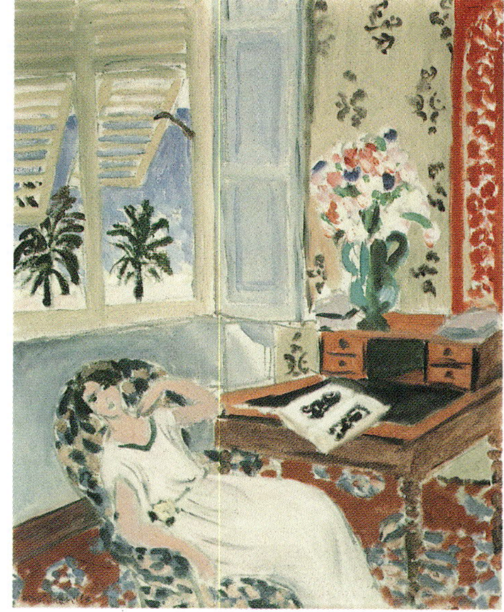

Matisse and the theme of the window

To paint is to reveal something, to invite the onlooker into a different space. That is why windows always fascinate painters. The artist's canvas is also a little like a window: it is either in a frame or, if it has not yet been framed, stretched across one. But what does it open on to?

After the invention of perspective in the 16th century, painters tried to make their work as close as possible to reality, to offer a kind of window on to the world. In fact the word perspective comes from the Latin *perspicere*, "to see through". Some painters, such as Leonardo da Vinci, Dürer and Poussin, invented complex mechanisms to project what they saw on to a flat surface. The problem was that they were acting as though everyone always sees the same thing. You need only ask two people to describe what they see through a window to prove the opposite. We all filter what we see through our own eyes, our brains and our whole beings.
There is never any truly objective picture. Nor is there an objective photograph, even if photography describes reality more faithfully. In 1942 Matisse wrote to his son, "the picture is not a mirror that reflects what I experienced while making it, but a powerful object, strong and expressive, that is as new to me as it is to anyone".

Portrait of Baroness Gourgaud (1924), Nice. Oil on canvas: 81 x 65 cm.

Is this really a portrait? Walls, doors, windows and mirrors invade the space; the figures may be seen from both front and back. Matisse is more interested in the space than in the figures. ▶

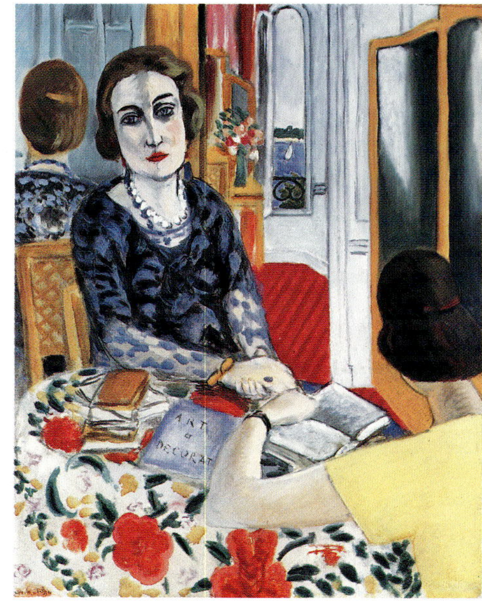

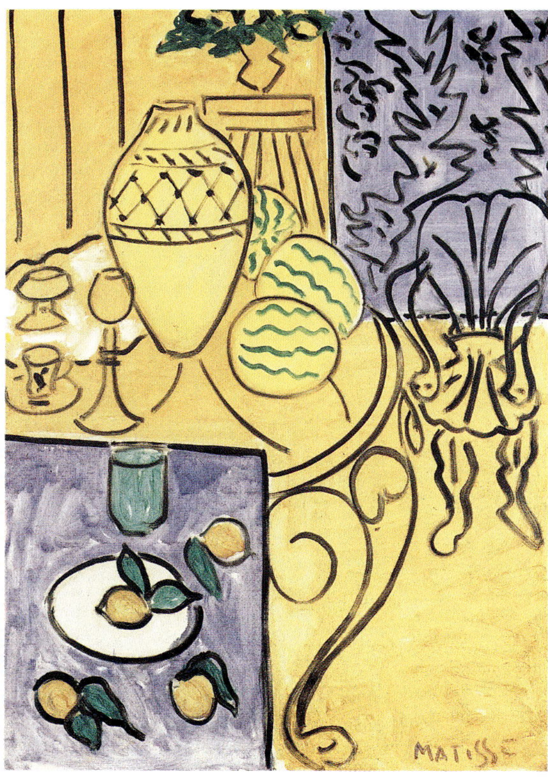

▲
Yellow and Blue Interior (1946), Vence. Oil on canvas: 116 x 81 cm.

Matisse painted many interiors in the 1920s. He returned to the theme between 1946 and 1948 with a dozen canvases. The window has disappeared, to be replaced by paintings within the painting.

Woman reading on a Black Background (August 1939), Paris. Oil on canvas: 92 x 73.5 cm. ▶

The photographer Brassaï was present when Matisse painted this scene. But he had difficulty recalling the setting: Matisse changed everything by adding a black background.

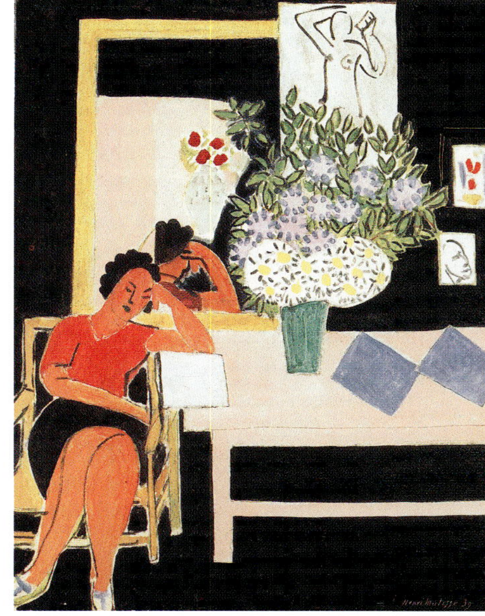

The theme of the window

A window is often present in Matisse's paintings because it represents a threshold between the inside and outside. It is through the window that daylight and night enter. Matisse sought out light more than any other painter; he found it in the Midi after he left his native Picardy. When he travelled, it was to look for what he lacked, another kind of light and a different space. Although Matisse loved to walk in the sun, he rarely painted out of doors. His favourite place was his studio, because there he found both shadow and light, and the line of demarcation between them, the window. Light, window and space, three elements that could not be disassociated.

Matisse painted large numbers of interiors and studios. They all have a window. Through them we may see an urban landscape – Paris and the banks of the Seine – or a garden, at Issy-les-Moulineaux or Vence, where he moved in 1943. In Collioure the windows open wide on to the sea with boats. In Nice the shutters are half-open, filtering the light.
In March 1942 a radio journalist asked Matisse about the charm of his paintings with open windows. "It probably comes," replied the painter, "from the fact that, as I feel it, space is all one from the horizon to the interior of my studio-bedroom, and the passing boat exists in the same space as the familiar objects around me; the window wall doesn't create two different worlds."

In the history of painting, windows have been primarily used to make a hole in the space of the picture and to give the illusion of another universe in which the onlooker can wander. Matisse gave the window a new role: to bring the outside into the painting. Matisse's window opens on to the painting.

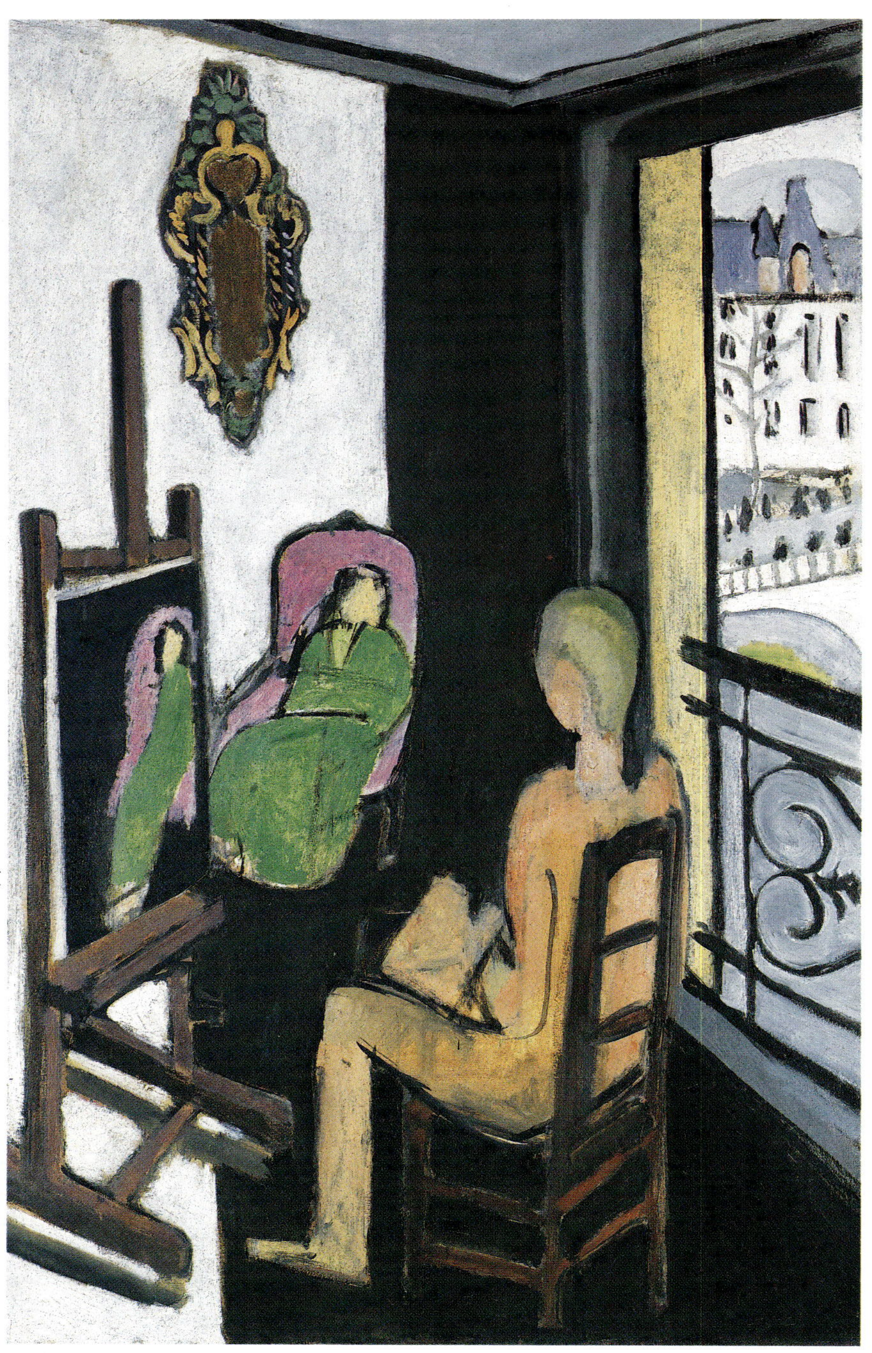

THE PAINTER IN HIS STUDIO

late 1916

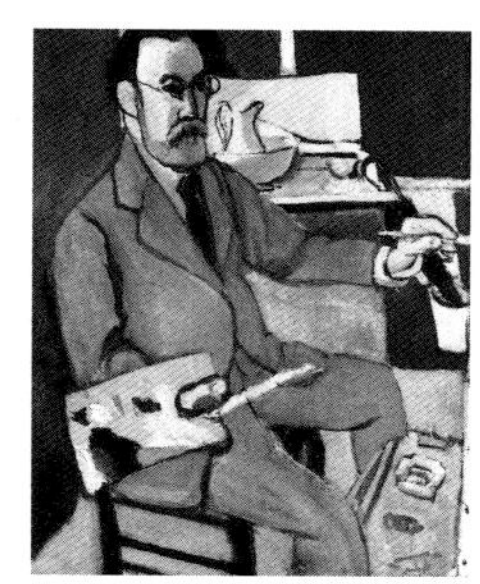

▲ *Self-portrait* (1918).
Oil on canvas:
65 x 54 cm.
Musée Matisse,
Le Cateau-Cambrésis.

A mirror without reflections, a transparent man, an easel floating against a wall: what a strange studio! Where is Matisse taking us?

Sadness and anxiety. For two years there had been war. Matisse wanted to enlist in the army. He was rejected. What could he do but go on painting?
Some months earlier he had found his first professional model, Laurette. She poses in the mauve armchair. Through a large window, blocked off by the picture's right-hand edge, we can see Paris, with a bridge over the Seine, though the river itself is invisible. A bare tree, washed-out colours – white, pale pink, grey-blue – it is winter.

the floor has disappeared!

This broad strip of washed-out colours echoes the studio's white wall. This wall is one with the floor, formed of the same flat block of colour. Floor, wall, outside, everything merges. Only a small section of grey ceiling, with its double diagonal lines, gives the room a classical perspective.
The painter is there, an ochre silhouette against the black wall. He sits motionless on his brown chair with a palette on his knees. He has broken off – or finished? – his work. This painter is Matisse, of course, looking at his model. The woman is also looking at him. Matisse has painted no details. How has he managed to express the intimacy between the painter and the model?

Matisse and his models
Why, at the age of 30, did Matisse insist on going to an art school studio? To find models. At first he worked with his wife, Amélie, then his daughter, Marguerite. In 1915 he started using professional models: Laurette (1915-17), Antoinette (1919-20), Henriette (1920-27). Lydia Delektorskaya was his secretary, his assistant, his companion and friend. At the end of his life he also worked with Monique Bourgeois, who later became a nun.

◀ *The Painter in his Studio* (late 1916), Paris.
Oil on canvas:
146.5 cm high,
97 cm wide.

why paint your studio?

The painter's studio. Matisse discovered this theme while working in Gustave Moreau's studio. The subject is as old as painting. In the religious paintings of the Renaissance, we sometimes see a saint painting the Virgin. In these pictures the studio window opens on to a magnificent landscape: paradise.
When 17th-century artists painted a studio, they showed one thing only, the creation of a painting. In *The Painter in his Studio* by the Dutch artist Vermeer, the painter has already moved to a chair and is seen from behind, facing his female model.
Often the painter will be alone in his studio, brush and palette in hand, painting his own portrait in front of a mirror. Rembrandt, Vermeer's contemporary, has left some astounding self-portraits. He did not paint

The studio and the window
The first studio scenes with a window appeared in the Middle Ages. At that time the painter was seen as an artisan and his studio was like a chemist's laboratory. In the 17th century, he became an important figure in society. His studio was then a fashionable subject for painting, particularly in Holland. In most paintings of interiors of this period, the light comes from the left. Studios were orientated towards the north, to avoid direct sunlight. To take advantage of the natural light, the painter would place his easel with the window to the left, to avoid casting the shadow of his right arm (if he was right-handed) on the canvas.

Jan Vermeer van Delft (1632-1775), *The Painter in his Studio* (c. 1665). Oil on canvas: 120 x 100 cm. Kunsthistorisches Museum, Vienna. ▶

The curtain is open on an intimate scene lit by the window on the left, which we cannot see.

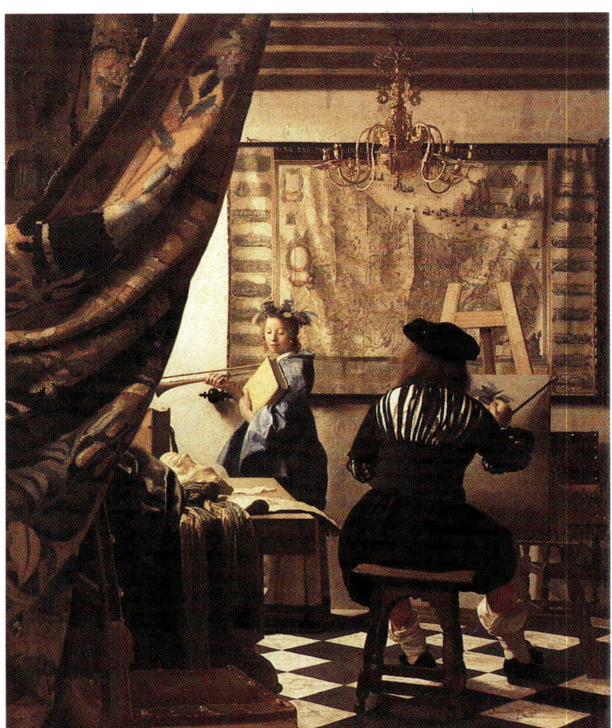

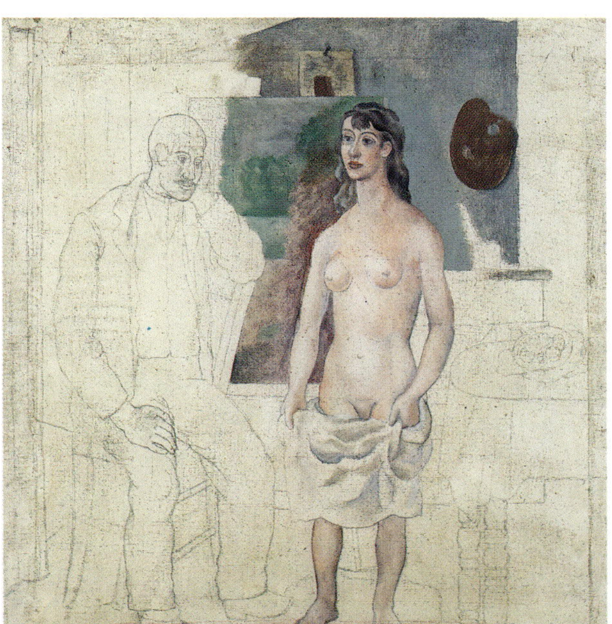

◄ **Pablo Picasso** (1881-1973) *The Painter and his Model* (summer 1914). Oil and pencil on canvas: 58 x 56 cm.

Only one thing is truly completed in this drawing/painting – the palette, symbol of the painter. The landscape and model are not quite finished. The artist himself is drawn in pencil, giving pride of place to his creation.

the window, the light source. All the same, the light in his pictures has such an intense quality that it seems to have come from another universe, the painter's inner world.

In the mid-19th century, Courbet painted a vast picture; in it he himself is enthroned in the middle of his studio. Does he take himself for the centre of the world? That was what the public thought, and was shocked. In fact, through this theme Courbet was asking a question to which he constantly returned: what role does the painter have in society?

spotlight on the model

For Matisse the question was different. He allotted himself a modest place, seen from behind, leaving us facing the model. His gaze, ours, the diagonal of the easel and that of the window's balustrade all converge on a single object, the seated woman. This interplay of lines has a corresponding interplay of colours, based on yellow ochre. There is ochre in the painter's silhouette, in the woman's face, in the mirror and also in the window. Why all these correspondences?

why a window on to Paris?

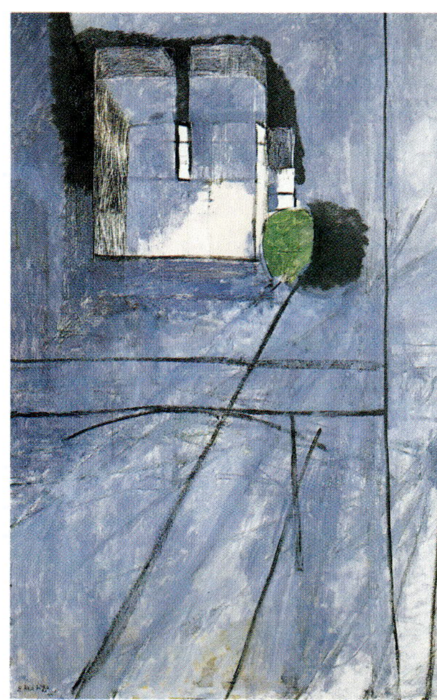

◄ *View of Notre-Dame* (1914). Oil on canvas: 147.3 x 94.3 cm. Museum of Modern Art, New York.

From his studio window Matisse could see the cathedral of Notre-Dame-de-Paris. Its massive shape seems to make a hole in the blue background. The black lines suggest the bridge and quayside. They lead to a green bouquet, the only allusion to nature.

From 1899 to 1907 Matisse lived in Paris at 19 Quai Saint-Michel. Early in 1914, before the start of World War I, he returned to spend the four years of the war there. He saw his painter friends, Marquet, Picasso, Gleizes and Gris, met some art critics and poets like Walter Pach, Max Jacob, Blaise Cendrars and Guillaume Apollinaire, and painted portraits of some of his admirers and patrons, including Sarah and Michael Stein, Greta Prozor and Auguste Pellerin. It was a very busy period for Matisse.

a question of transparency

At that time Matisse began to paint studios with, oddly, a goldfish bowl. For the painter this was highly symbolic. Its transparent surface contained a different universe – the closed world of the fish. We are in the same room and yet we are excluded from that other world, we are outside it.

The window has something of the goldfish bowl about it. It is also a transparent surface and it brings the landscape into the room. It brings the outside into the inside. In *The Painter in his Studio*, there is one other important element, the Venetian mirror. What is the point of this large mirror, hung high on the wall, reflecting nothing? Artists do not need a mirror to reflect the world – that is what Matisse is saying. Nor do they need to give the details of a face; an outline is enough. The painter is not showing us a real work-place in this picture. He is showing us the place where creation happens, his own secret garden.

Matisse and Paris
In 1887 Matisse went to Paris to study law. He returned in 1891 to study art. In February 1899 he moved there with his family, to the banks of the Seine, on the fifth floor of 19 Quai Saint-Michel. At the end of 1907 he opened an academy at the Des Oiseaux convent (on the corner of the Boulevard du Montparnasse and the Rue de Sèvres). Barely a year later he moved his academy to the Hôtel Biron. In 1909 he rented, then bought a house in the suburbs, at Issy-les-Moulineaux. In December 1913 he returned to 19 Quai Saint-Michel, one floor lower down. After 1917 Matisse usually spent the winter in Nice but returned to Paris from May to September. Around 1928 he bought a flat at 132 Boulevard du Montparnasse.

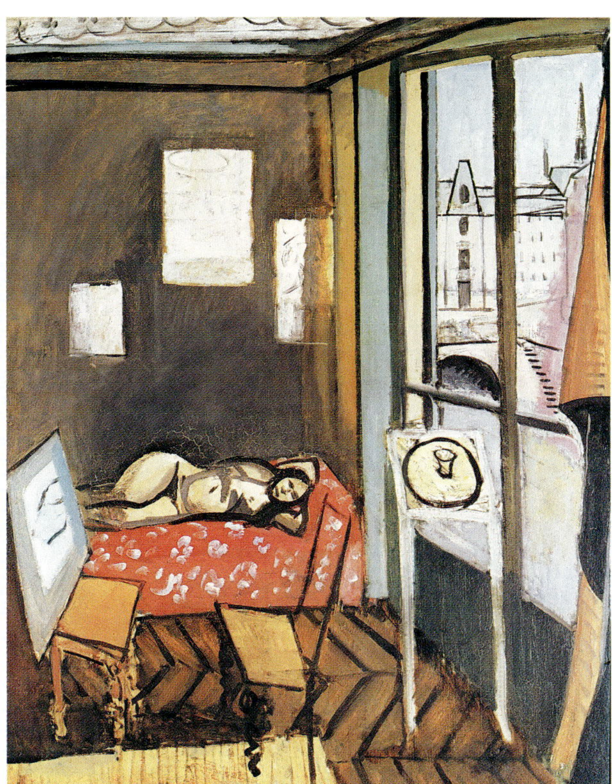

◄ *The Studio, Quai Saint-Michel* (1916). Oil on canvas: 146 x 116 cm. The Phillips Collection, Washington.

The painter has departed, leaving his chair empty. The beginnings of a painting face the window, like an echo. The two are linked by the body of a woman lying down, reminiscent of the bridge outside.

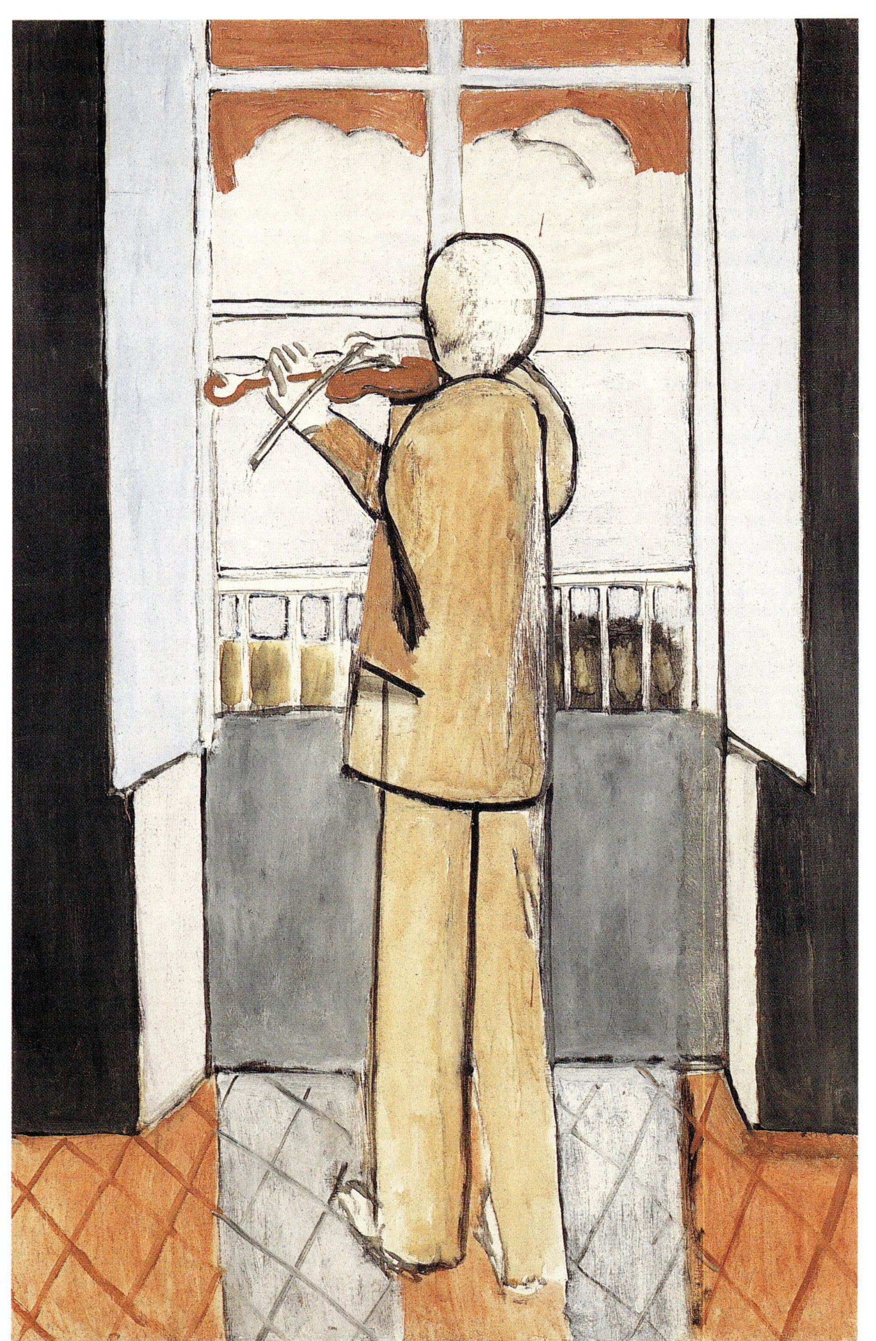

THE VIOLINIST AT THE WINDOW

spring 1918

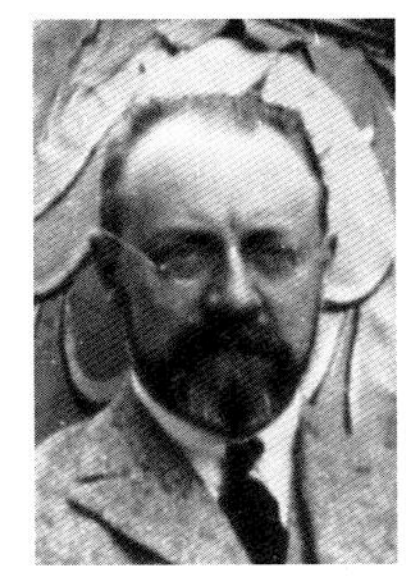

▲ Photograph of Matisse in 1920.

During his first winter in Nice, in 1917, Matisse lived alone in a hotel room. He had set up his studio in a nearby apartment. Was it because he needed to be alone that he painted this strange, sad picture?

No other work by Matisse had ever been constructed with so many verticals! The overall look is created using two areas of black wall, blue-ish shutters, the bars of the balustrade and two strips of grey on the floor. Verticality is reinforced by the violinist, a long silhouette framed by the window. The whole is however broken up by a few horizontal lines in the centre.

head in the clouds

At the bottom of the picture, a change of colour separates wall from floor. The floor is not seen from the same angle as the rest of the room. The tiles are shown from a high angle, as though we were looking down at our feet, whereas the window seems to be directly in front of us. The man in the centre is faceless and ageless. With his head the colour of the clouds and his violin parallel to the window frame, he seems about to fade into the surroundings. Without the thick black line that outlines him, he would have no existence other than as a geometric shape. Matisse has completed his universe with a few sparse diagonals, such as the one of which the bow is a part. Is this simply to break the rhythm, or is it to help us enter into the picture and hear the violinist?

◀ *The Violinist at the Window* (spring 1918), Nice. Oil on canvas: 150 cm high, 98 cm wide.

seven notes on Matisse's palette

"You must paint the way you sing, without constraints". He certainly sang the tune of the farandole to find inspiration for *The Dance*. Unlike Picasso, who had no ear for music, Matisse could not do without it.
At the end of 1914 he took violin lessons and bought the instrument we see in his pictures. In 1915 he decided that Pierre, his younger son then aged 15, should abandon school for nine hours of violin per day and a bit of piano, between six and eight o'clock in the morning.
When war came Pierre enlisted in the cavalry. In 1918 he told his father that he wanted to become an art

▲ *The Violinist* (1917). Charcoal on canvas: 194 x 114 cm. Musée Matisse, Le Cateau-Cambrésis.

Matisse's children, Pierre and Marguerite, visited their father in Nice in the winter of 1918. Matisse began a portrait of Pierre as a violinist. This sketch was to become *The Violinist at the Window*.

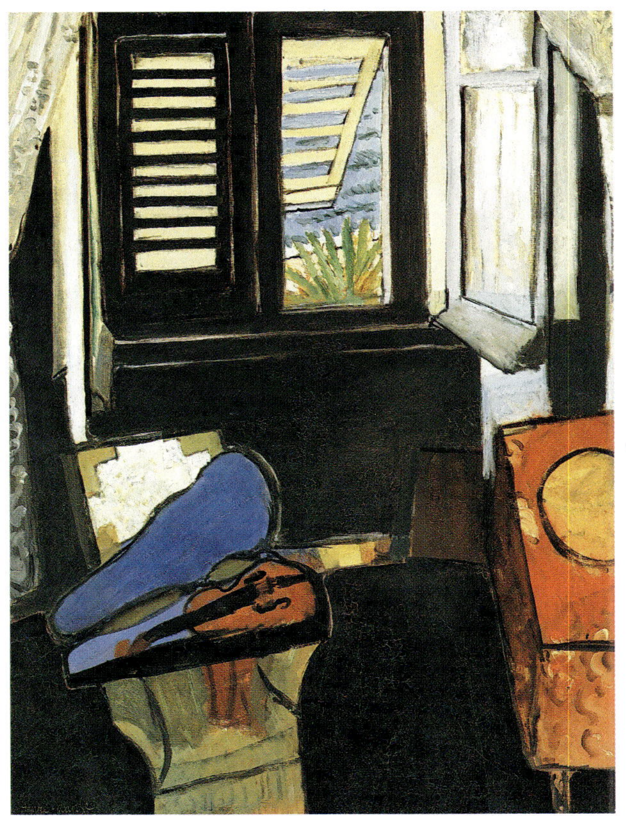

◄ *Interior with a Violin* (1917-18). Oil on canvas: 116 x 89 cm. Statens Museum for Kunst, Copenhagen.

Here we find the same black and the same rigorous construction as in *The Violinist at the Window*. The eye is drawn to the violin case, bluer than the sea.

Pierre Matisse, art dealer
In 1925 Pierre Matisse organised his first exhibition, in New York, with lithographs by his father. Two years later he exhibited French avant-garde painting. Pierre became one of the most important gallery owners in New York.

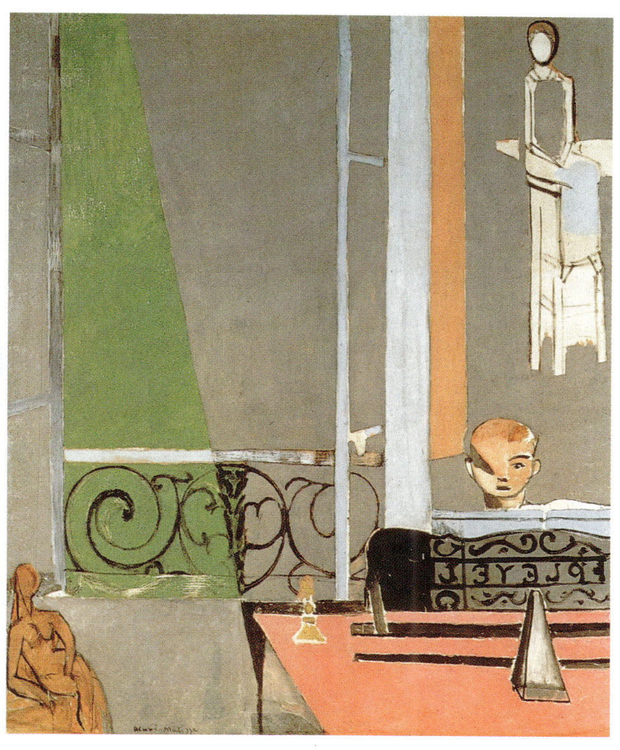

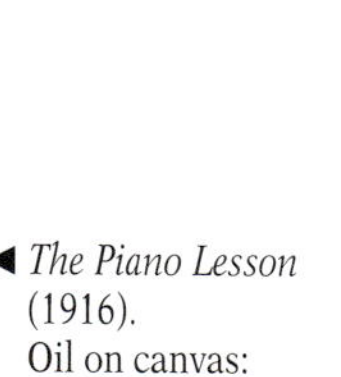

◄ *The Piano Lesson* (1916). Oil on canvas: 245 x 212.5 cm. Museum of Modern Art, New York.

In 1916 Matisse's second son, Pierre, was 16. Here he is, made to appear younger by his father, looking over the piano. Like the window, the shadow on his forehead carries an echo of the metronome on the piano.

Matisse and Cubism
Between 1913, when he returned from Morocco, and 1917, when he moved to Nice, Matisse simplified his forms and colours. No doubt the war led him to this restraint. More importantly, he was interested in Cubism, a new movement, whose great masters were Picasso and Juan Gris. But Matisse never painted like these two, who abandoned reality for the world of abstraction.

dealer. Matisse was terribly disappointed. He so much wanted his son to be a musician, or even a painter or sculptor.

Matisse was not the only 20th-century artist to link painting and music. In 1926 the painter Kandinsky, who also taught at the famous German art school, the Bauhaus, published a book called *Point and line to plane*. He observed that the same terms were used in painting and music – line, note, stroke, harmony – and compared the volume of a sound to the thickness of a line. Like Kandinsky, Matisse could not talk about painting without talking about music. "Of course music and colour have nothing in common", he acknowledged in 1945, "but they follow parallel paths. Seven notes with slight modifications are enough to write any score. Why should the same not be true of painting?" Black, white, grey, blue, red, pink and brown: there are seven colours in *The Violinist at the Window*. Is this a simple coincidence?

a new way of painting light

During World War I, Matisse's compositions were rigorous and in dark colours. However in *The Violinist at the Window* his colours are paler and his touch lighter: he uses oil paint a little like watercolour, playing with transparency. Why? He was attempting to convey the silvery light of Nice.
Early in 1918 his painter friend Renoir told him: "When you put a black on the canvas, it stays where it is. But all my life I've thought that you couldn't use it without breaking up the chromatic unity of the surface."
This was Matisse's secret: he was not afraid of black. He used it like real colour, which had been an unusual practice since the time of the Impressionists. Once again, by refusing to imitate reality, Matisse was setting off on a new path. "You can invoke light

Matisse and Bonnard
At first sight Matisse and Bonnard had nothing in common. Yet both travelled and finally met up in the Midi light they needed so much. Through their letters, published in 1991, we learn of their mutual admiration and of the friendship between these two loners who were united by a single passion, painting.

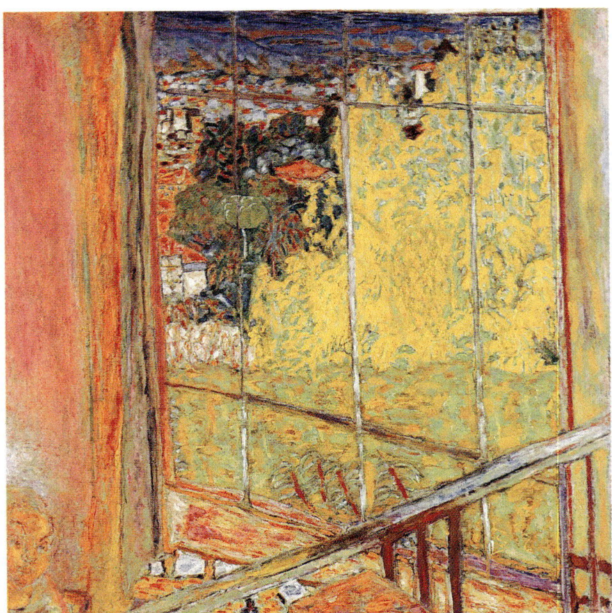

Pierre Bonnard ►
(1867-1946)
Studio with Mimosa
(1939-46).
Oil on canvas:
127.5 x 127.5 cm.

The yellow of the flowers floods Bonnard's studio. This painter was as drawn as his friend Matisse to the theme of the window.

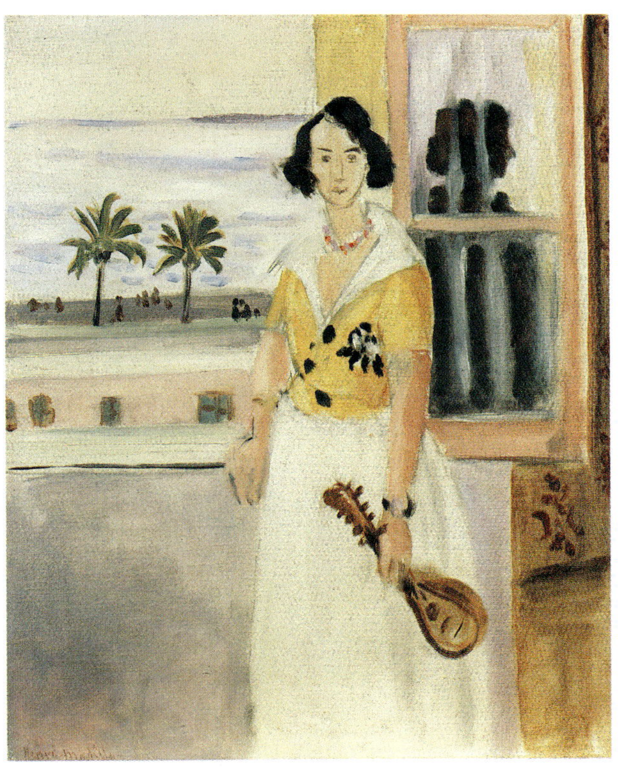

◄ *Woman with a Mandolin* (1922). Oil on canvas: 47 x 40 cm. Musée de l'Orangerie, Walter Guillaume collection, Paris.

Many themes are combined here: outside and inside, window and mirror, woman and musical instrument, light and darkness, painting and music. It was in Nice in 1920s that Matisse was most interested in windows.

A red sky
A patch of blue tends to darken; it would be easier, more sensible, perhaps more beautiful, to convey impalpable, distant things, particularly the sky, using red, orange and yellow, and to use blue for solid, compact, close elements. Charles Lapicque (20th-century painter and theorist), *Essai sur l'espace, l'art et la destinée* ("Essay on space, art and destiny"), Grasset, 1958.

by the invention of flat colour, like you use chords in music," he said to Gaston Diehl, in 1947. "You're not a slave to blue, green or red". This is how Matisse did without yellow to render light, by using black.

a disguised self-portrait

The Violinist at the Window is Matisse himself. A lone, ethereal man facing another world. As in *The Painter in his Studio*, he seems to be looking outside. But this time he is so close, he merges so far into this window, that he seems to be near to reaching his goal: "Doing with painting what I've done with drawing – getting into the picture without contradiction, like into the bunch of flowers in that photograph you sent me," he wrote to his son Pierre.

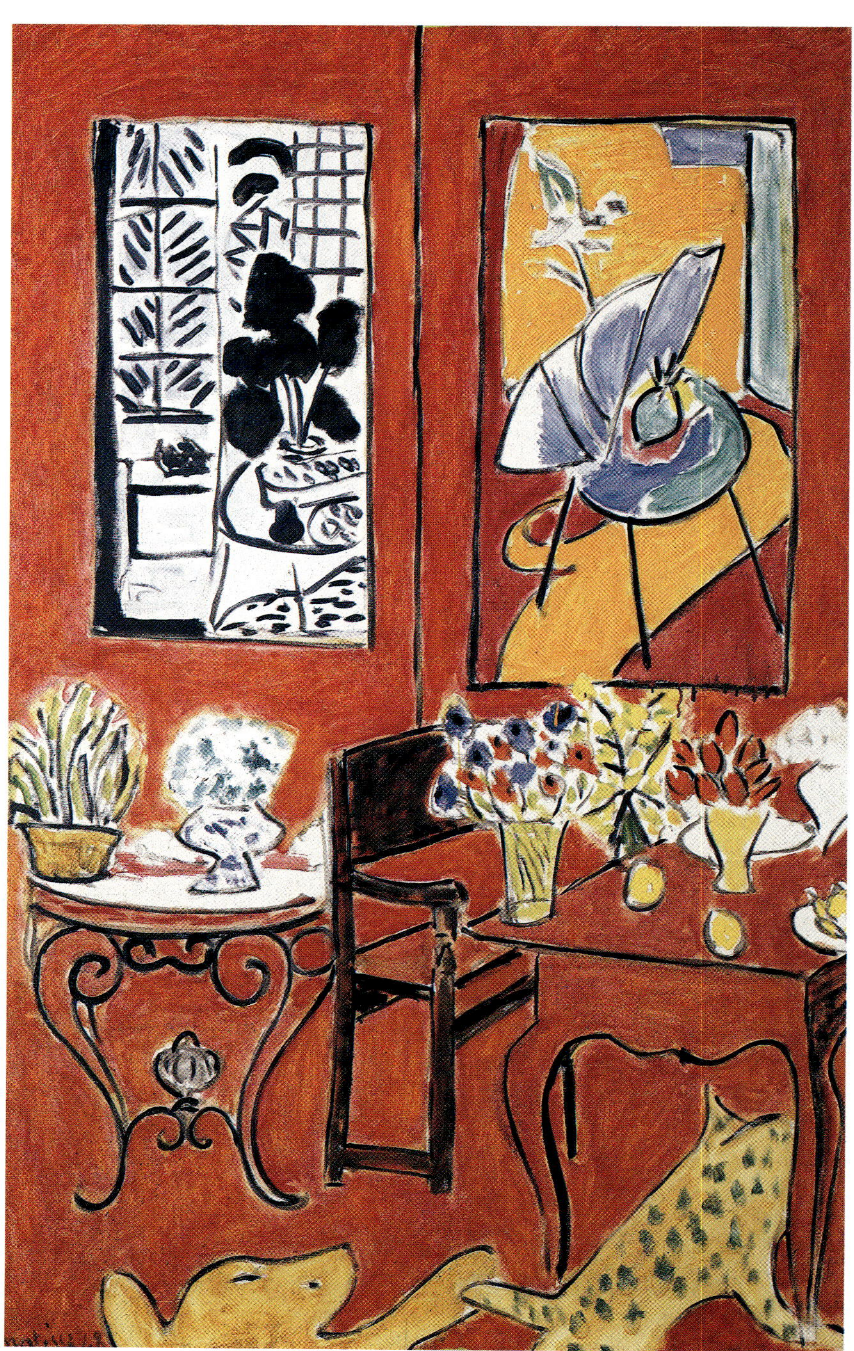

LARGE RED INTERIOR

1948

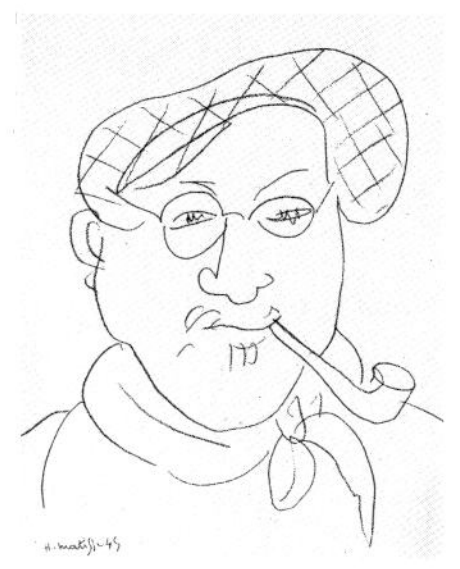

▲ *Self-portrait* (1945). Pencil on paper: 41.8 x 32.3 cm. Private collection.

Is this an ordinary interior scene? No. In this *Large Red Interior* we find all the themes that have obsessed Matisse.

Two tables: a rectangular one, which might be made of wood if it were not red like the floor and walls, and a round one, smaller, with wrought iron legs and a top of white marble (or rather canvas!). Under the right-hand table are two yellow rugs, cut off, like the table, by the edge of the picture. Or are they in fact two dogs, chasing each other? There are flowers on the tables. The one on the left has two pots, one containing a houseplant; the table on the right has two vases of flowers – blue and red anemones in a transparent yellow vase and red tulips in an opaque yellow vase. Behind them we can vaguely see two other bunches.

You have to be decorative; expression and decoration are one and the same thing. Henri Matisse.

two and two makes a picture

Also on the large table are two white plates, one empty, the other piled with lemons. Two more lemons have slipped off the plate. In the centre of the picture is a chair. Above it a black line rises vertically from the middle of the chair's back, cutting the space in two. Higher up and on either side of this line, are two pictures of interiors. The black and white picture is also cut in half vertically. In the coloured picture are the same round table, the same red background and the same yellow carpet. So can this be an ordinary interior, when there are so many pairs?

◀ *Large Red Interior* (1948), Vence. Oil on canvas: 146 x 97 cm.

why such a fascination with objects?

Matisse always liked the intimate space of interiors. In 1896, in *Interior with a Top Hat*, he painted an empty armchair, a desk covered in objects and paintings on the walls. In a series of studio pictures done in 1911, he once more decorated his walls with pictures containing brightly coloured plant and flower motifs.

Late in his life Matisse rediscovered the objects around him. In 1943 he had gone to Vence, a few kilometres from Nice, to get away from the shelling. Vence was a perfect place to retire for a 79-year-old man who was world-famous, rich and had received the Legion d'Honneur. He loved his garden, his flowers and the terrace with its enormous palm tree. But in fact, "rest is torture," he said; "you need an awful lot of courage to do nothing". Matisse had not been painting much in the preceding years. After an operation for intestinal

What does red symbolise?
Red draws the eye more than blue because it reflects longer light waves. It is the most shocking colour, symbolising fire and anger, but also love. According to the German poet Goethe, red stimulates the imagination. In the Middle Ages it was the colour of Christ. This was partly because of his spilt blood, of course, but also, according to the theologian Raban Maur, because it symbolised "the purity of light". Divine light could thus be represented in either blue or crimson.

Hélène Adant, ►
The studio in Vence (1946). Photograph.

In 1943 Matisse moved to Vence, to his villa Le Rêve ("The Dream"). This photo shows the round table of *Large Red Interior*, which was in fact a view of Matisse's studio.

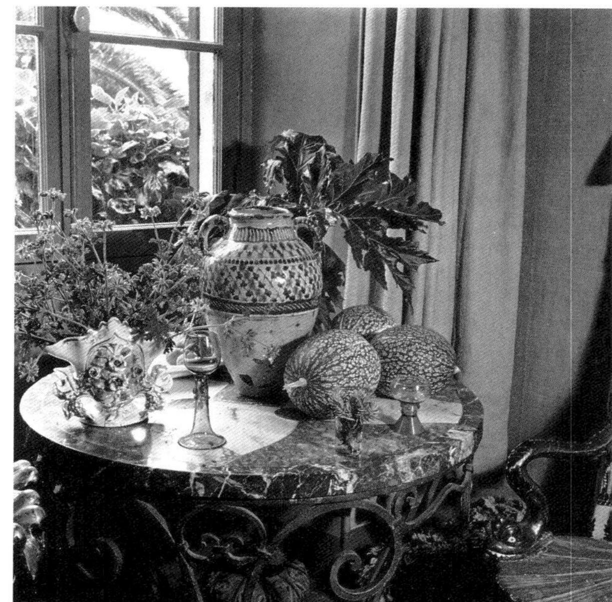

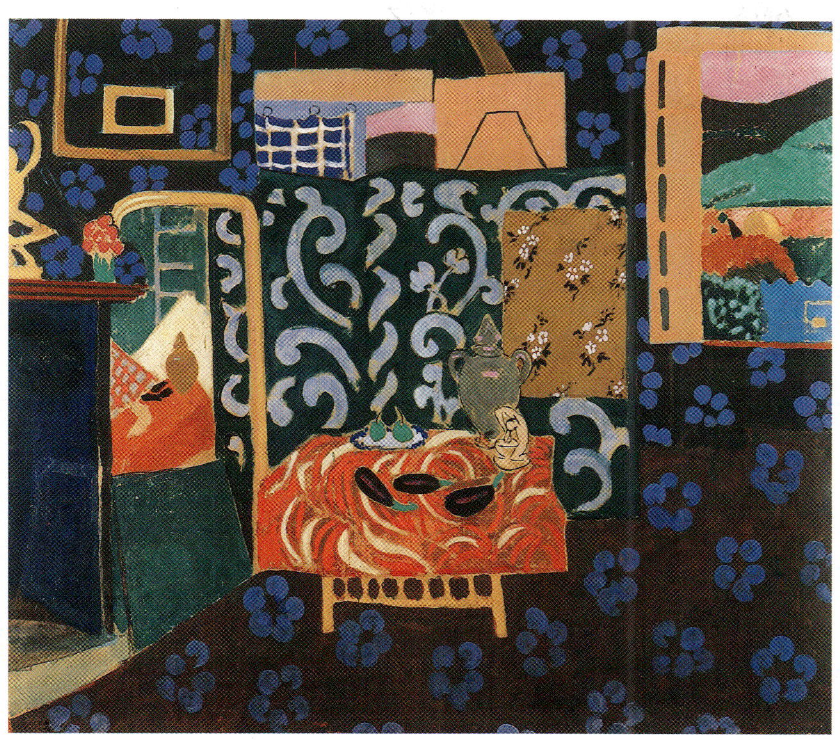

◄ *Interior with Aubergines* (1911). Tempera with glue on linen canvas: 212 x 244 cm. Musée des Beaux-Arts, Grenoble.

The first series of interiors appeared in 1911. Here again a window appears to the right and a mirror on the left. But the profusion of decorative elements on the floor, wall and screen confuse what we see.

Balancing colours
At the 1908 Autumn Salon exhibition, the Russian collector Shchukin bought a *Blue Table* by Matisse. But what a surprise! The table came to him entirely repainted in red. This was the well-known *Red Table*. Matisse's explanation? Balancing the colour.

cancer in 1941, he found it hard to remain sitting or standing for long and could only work for two hours a day. Instead he drew constantly.

a journey to the land of red

In 1946 he took up his brush again. A year later he wrote to his friend André Rouveyre: "I am definitively involved in colour, as drawings don't interest me any more [....] I've got several canvases under way. I feel all the curiosity that a new country gives you, as I've never been so far advanced in the expression of my colours."

Art and decoration
"It is the characteristic of modern art to be part of our life".

what is the picture hiding?

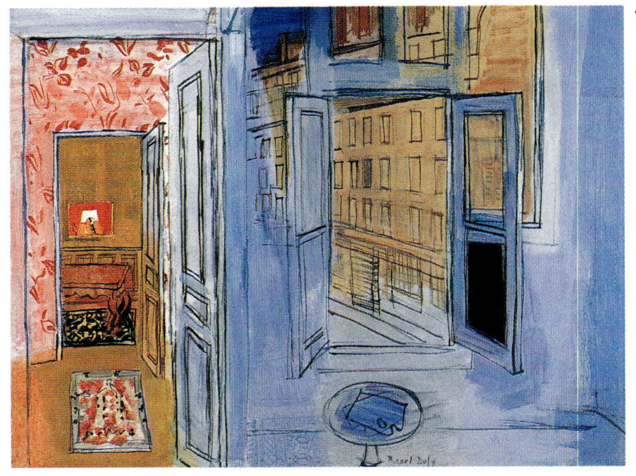

◀ **Raoul Dufy** (1877-1953), *The Studio in Impasse Guelma* (1935-52). Oil on canvas: 89 x 117 cm.

A series of doors draws the eye towards the interior, while the city seems to come in through the open window. How is this possible? The answer lies in the palette on the round table – through painting.

The *Large Red Interior* was a corner of Matisse's studio. The two pictures on the wall really exist. Matisse painted the *Interior with Window and Palm Tree*, on the left, and *The Pineapple*, on the right, in 1948. The picture on the left shows the view over the terrace, with its palm tree, and acts like a window. The one on the right echoes the colours and objects shown in the *Large Red Interior*.

a black vertical line right in the middle...

In Matisse's studio these two pictures hung on different walls. This is why Matisse painted a vertical line that splits the space in two: it symbolises the corner where the walls meet. In this painter's world a vertical line is always used to add precision to shapes, even to curves. The arabesque curls round a vertical line.
By doubling up the objects, Matisse brings opposites together – straight lines and curves, rectangles and

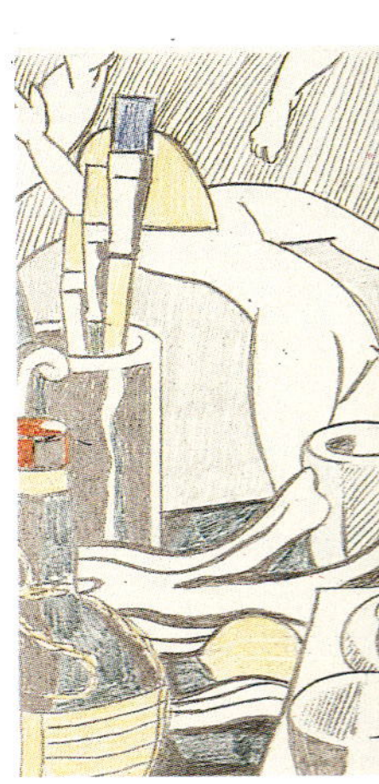

Roy Lichtenstein ▶ (born 1923), *The Artist's Studio* (1974). Coloured crayon on paper: 56.5 x 38 cm. Private collection.

This picture, by the leading exponent of Pop Art, was part of a series of studio views dedicated to Matisse. The picture in the background recalls *The Dance* and, in the still-life, are the lemons of *Large Red Interior*.

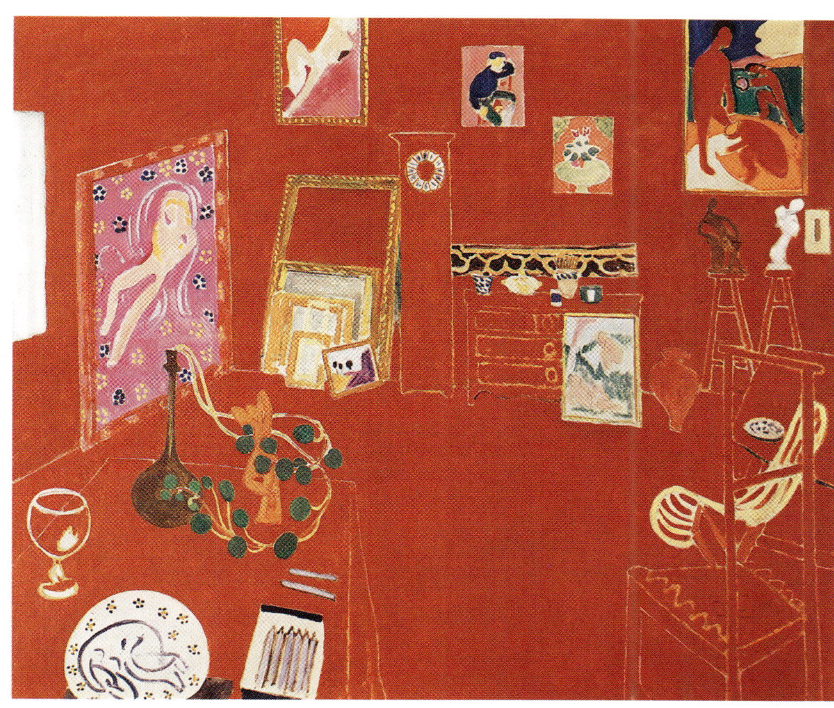

◀ *The Red Studio* (1911). Oil on canvas: 181 x 219.1 cm. Museum of Modern Art, New York.

Matisse put red everywhere: *The Red Table* (1908), this *Red Studio* (1911), *The Goldfish* (called *Poisson rouge* – red fish – in French) (1912). As in *Large Red Interior*, red forms the wall, floor and furniture. It is so intense you feel you can still see its light when you close your eyes.

circles, painting and drawing, metal and wood, the transparent and the opaque, the empty and the full.

...and a single chair

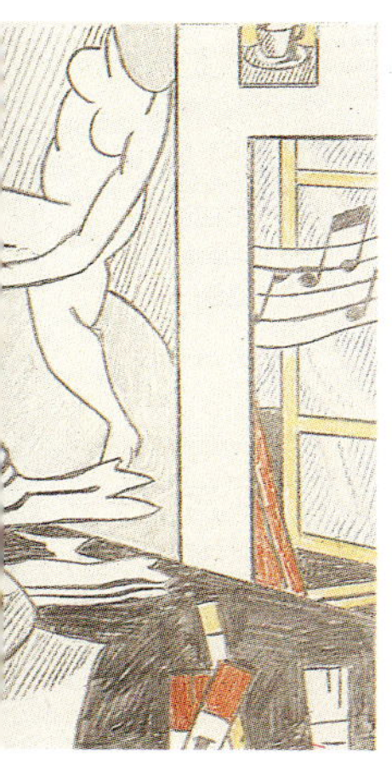

Yet one object remains single, the chair. Placed in the centre of the composition, it becomes the axis around which the twinned elements gravitate and the perspective is constructed. This chair symbolises Matisse's presence. All that we see has passed through the filter of his sensibility.

The themes dear to his heart recur here, as in a conclusion – colourful bunches of flowers and plants, and just like the sunny yellow lemons stand for still-life, the picture in black and white represents a landscape and even a woman is suggested by the drawing of arabesques. The window alone has disappeared, since Matisse has finally entered his painting.

The Colour Mediterranean, *a* poem dedicated to Matisse by André Verdet.

Perfect red crime
blood crying joy
oh lovely knife
my song
a murderer big enough
to commit
more happiness
more reasons
in red succession.

Illustration for *Les Jockeys camouflés & Période hors-texte* ("The camouflaged jockeys" and "A time outside the text") by Pierre Reverdy, 1918. Paris, printer Paul Birault. 27.5 x 19.5 cm. 48 pages. ►

Matisse and Reverdy met at Le Bateau-Lavoir.

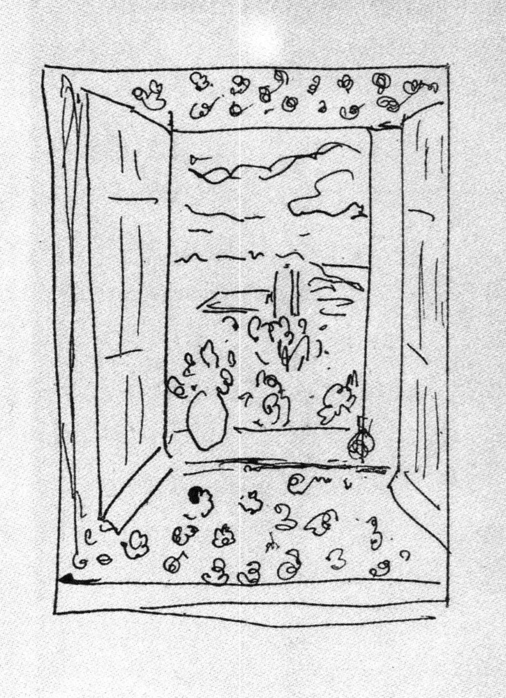

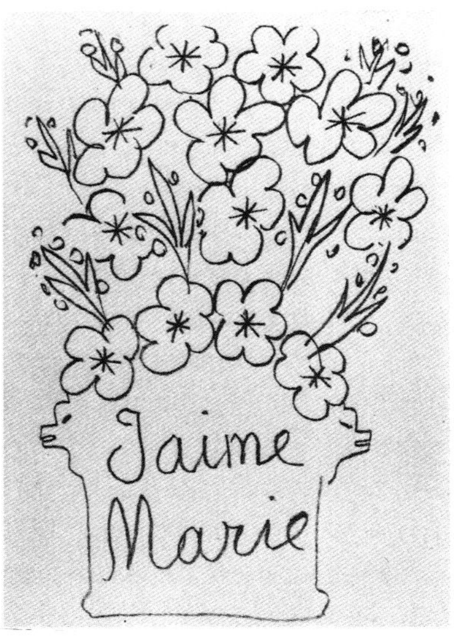

▲
Illustrated title page for *Le Florilège des amours* ("The anthology of love") by Ronsard, 1948. Paris, Albert Skira. 38 x 29 cm.

It took Matisse six years to illustrate this book. He also chose the typeface.

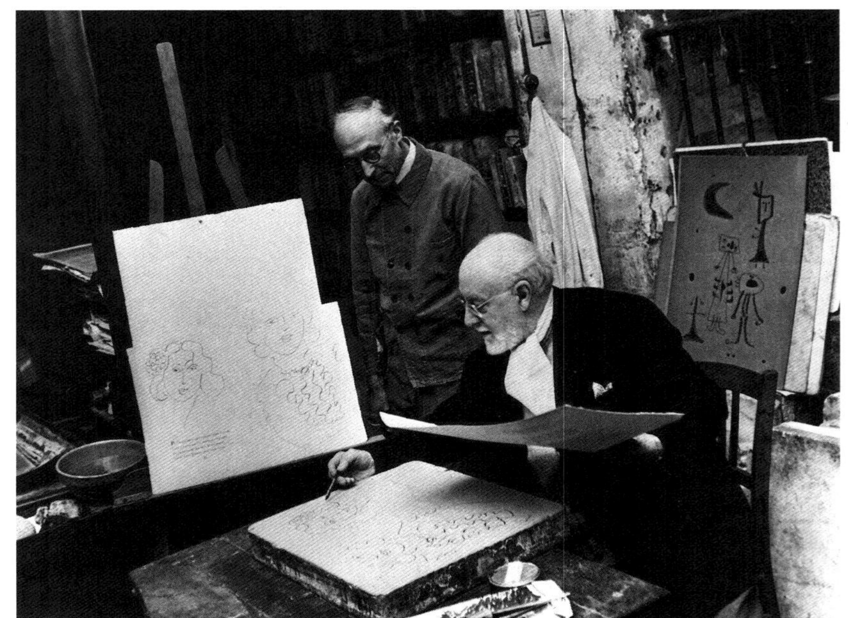

Matisse in the Mourlots' studio. ►

The Mourlot Brothers' studio produced the 20th-century's most prestigious lithographs, those of Chagall, Picasso and Matisse.

Matisse: writing and the image

Very early on Matisse wanted to illustrate the writings he loved. In 1918 he gave five drawings to Pierre Reverdy to print in his *Camouflaged jockeys*. These were not yet illustrations, since the drawings were not done to accompany the poems. In 1932 the Swiss publisher Albert Skira asked him to illustrate Mallarmé's *Poésies*. Matisse found the text powerful and thought hard about what he should express in the drawings. For illustrating a text does not mean reproducing it in images; it means speaking of the same subject and the same feelings in another language.
He chose line-engraving on copper plate. The copper is covered with a varnish, which enables the artist to avoid marking the metal directly, barely touching it instead. Matisse liked this technique, which gave him a thin, regular line.
To ensure perfect harmony between image and text, he also chose the typeface in which the poem would be printed.

Other techniques besides line-engraving make it possible to play with the contrast between text and image. Engraving on linoleum – linocutting – gives a white line on a black background; and the page beside the image seems entirely white. Matisse liked using both linocuts and wood engraving, which he chose to illustrate Montherlant's *Pasiphaé*. However, to avoid the funereal appearance of black and white, he introduced red for the lettering and blue for the cover. This work kept him busy for ten months "throughout the day and often the night".

▶ Illustration for *Les Fleurs du mal* ("The flowers of evil") by Charles Baudelaire, 1947. Paris, La Bibliothèque française. 28.6 x 23 cm, 171 pages.

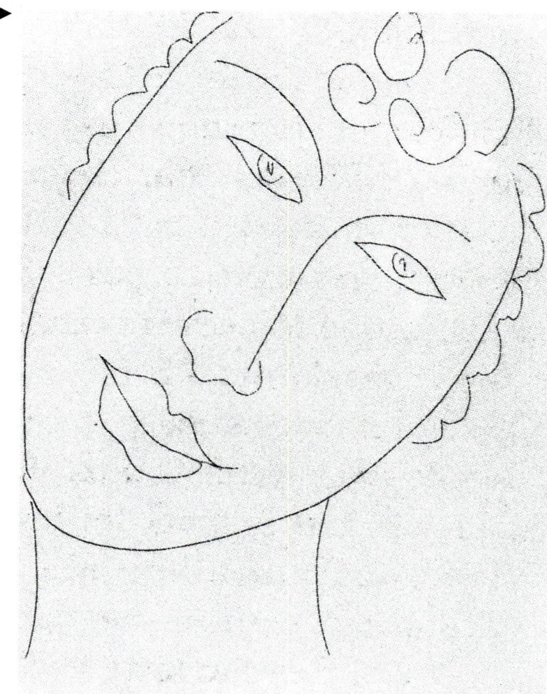

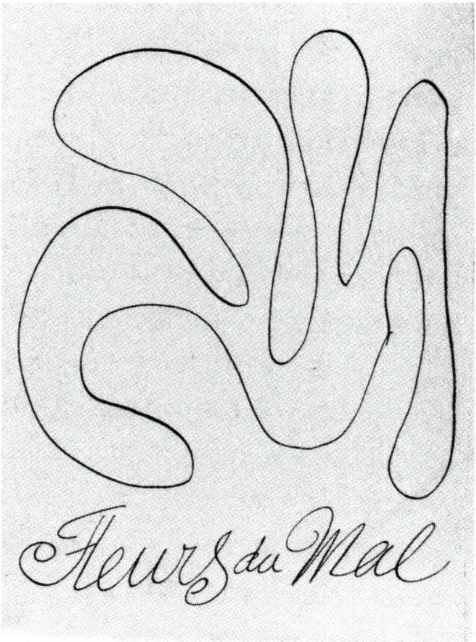

▲ Illustration for *Les Fleurs du mal* by Charles Baudelaire, 1947.

In a single continuous line Matisse drew the outline of a leaf. But between its lobes a new shape appears, inspired by Eastern art.

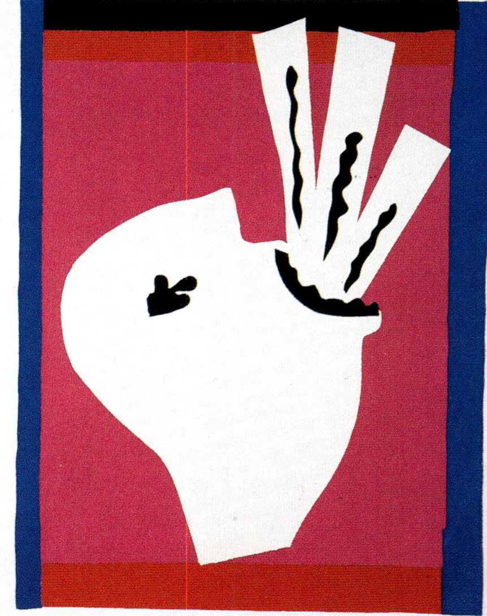

"The Sword Swallower", plate XIII of *Jazz,* 1943-46. Gouache on paper, cut out and stuck on paper glued on canvas: 43.3 x 34.3 cm.

Matisse was then asked to illustrate *La Rose des sables* ("The rose of the sands"), another work by Montherlant, but he soon realised that he would not be able to do it; some books leave no room for another language. Designing a stage set, doing the cartoon for a tapestry, illustrating books – all that is part of the work of 20th-century artists. Painters as famous as Picasso, André Masson and Juan Gris became prolific illustrators, mainly working with contemporary authors. Matisse preferred classical literature. He felt very sympathetic to the "flowery" language of such French poets of the Middle Ages as Charles d'Orléans and Pierre Ronsard.

In 1941 Matisse abandoned the idea of publishing his memoirs, *Mémoires de peintre*, promised to his publisher Albert Skira. Instead he suggested illustrating *Le Florilège des amours* ("The anthology of love") by Ronsard. The book came out six years later.
At that time Matisse was concentrating on drawing. He therefore chose to illustrate Ronsard with an allied technique, that of lithography. In this process the artist draws with a greasy bistre crayon on a limestone plate.
He planned 30 illustrations, but completed 136. He made numerous sketches for each one, particularly the floral motif that accompanies the poems dedicated to Marie. The printing was done by the Mourlot Studio, Matisse's favourite printer, and he supervised the whole process very closely.

Matisse had a special relationship with publishers. In winter 1937 Tériade asked for a cover for the first issue of *Verve*, an art magazine he was launching. Matisse produced his first cut-outs in three pure colours: red, blue and black. After perfecting the technique, he did more for the cover of issue no. 13 of April 1945.
In 1941 Tériade suggested producing a book in colour, a kind of "manuscript of modern paintings". Two years later, Matisse set to work. He was to produce the most extraordinary of all illustrated books – entitled *Jazz*.

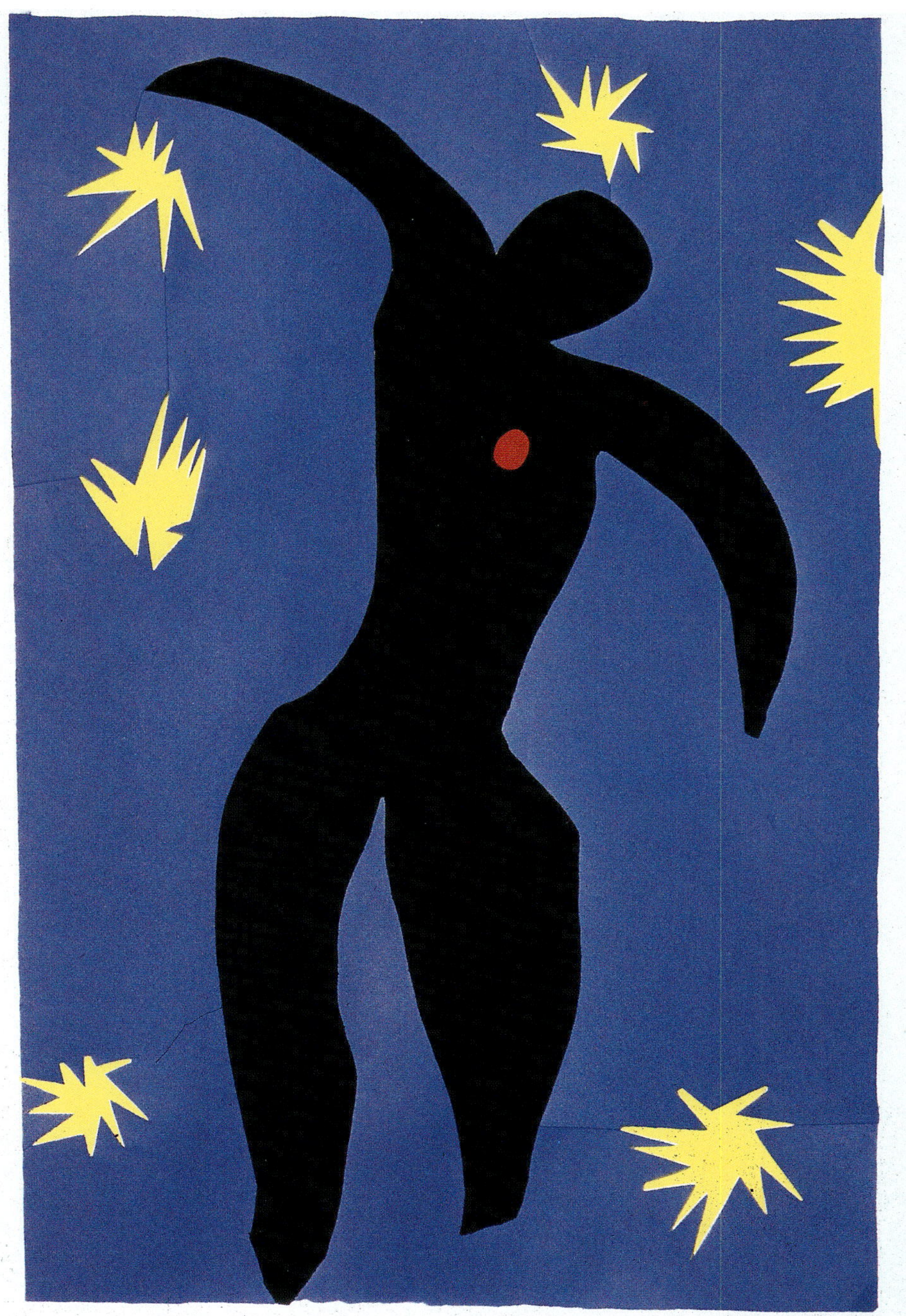

JAZZ
1943-47

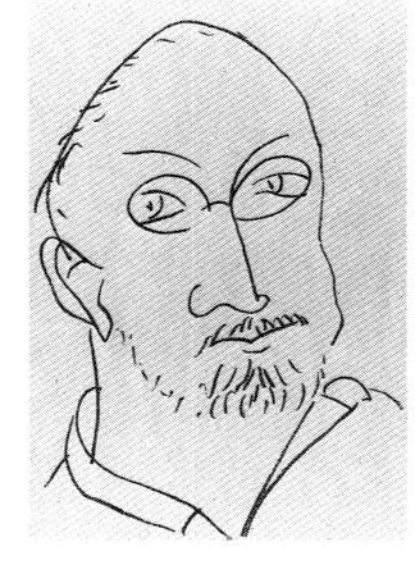

▲
Large Mask (1944).
Lithograph:
35.2 x 22 cm.
Bibliothèque
Nationale, Paris.

Matisse could no longer paint. Illness forced him to stay in bed. But this was not a real problem! To produce his book *Jazz*, he invented a new way of playing with colours, without using paints or brushes.

Coloured paper
Paper cut-outs are coloured drawings whose only aim is to use fine, ready-made colours, without disturbing their purity.
Matisse.

People said that he came "back from the dead". He recovered slowly from an operation he had had in 1941. A young nurse, Monique Bourgeois, looked after him. Gradually she became his model and assistant. She prepared the sheets of coloured paper, laying the gouache on the paper, and the artist worked the scissors.

cut and paste

For "Icarus", plate VIII of *Jazz*, he cut out a black shape, which he stuck on a sheet of intense, deep ultramarine: is it sky or sea? This technique had one big advantage – the clarity of line accentuated the contrast between colours.
Simply by its presence, the figure gives meaning to the background sheet of blue: this is the sky, with its six stars of different size and shape, cut from a sheet covered in a saturated, radiant yellow. The bird-man glides, arms outstretched, across the starry heavens. The yellow and blue are so luminous that, in contrast, the black shape seems to be falling away into the depths. To keep it in the foreground, Matisse once again used colour: the vermilion shape in the position of the heart seems to pierce the canvas.

◀ "Icarus", plate VIII of *Jazz*, 1943. Gouache on paper, cut out and stuck to paper stuck on canvas: 43.4 cm high, 43.1 cm wide.

Blue: a profound colour
Blue, a cold colour, distances objects from the eye. It is generally associated with the sky and sea, but also with night, cold, solitude and death. It marks the work of a number of painters: Van Gogh, who contrasted it with yellow; Picasso (between 1901 and 1904); Kandinsky and Franz Marc (around 1911 in Germany), who founded the Expressionist movement "Der Blaue Reiter" ("The Blue Horseman"); Yves Klein, who patented his famous ultramarine in 1960, not to be confused with "Monory blue", invented by Jacques Monory.

Matisse discovers boundless space

It's all so simple! A few snips with the scissors and three primary colours plus black are enough to tell the story of Icarus, the bird-man. Blue, for example, represents both sky and sea, in which Icarus drowned.

drunk on air

In 1937 Matisse left London by plane. This was his first trip through the air: what a revelation! So, above the greyness and worries, the sun really does always shine in boundless space...
After his exciting experience, the painter could not forget this intoxicating feeling of freedom. His perception of space – and of life – was forever transformed. For the bed-ridden artist, Icarus conveyed that same feeling.

Who was Icarus?
According to Greek mythology, Icarus was the son of Dedalus, architect of the famous Cretan labyrinth. When King Minos heard that his prisoners had escaped from the labyrinth, he punished Dedalus, imprisoning him there with his son. Dedalus used wax to make wings to escape. Before setting off, he warned Icarus not to fly too high; the wax could melt in the heat of the sun. Once in the air, Icarus forgot this advice. His wings came off, he fell and was drowned.

Georges Braque (1882-1963), *The Birds* (1949-51). Oil on canvas: 347 x 501 cm. Ceiling of the Etruscan Hall, the Louvre, Paris. Opened in 1953.

Two black birds against the blue of the sky. In choosing the theme of flight, Braque was returning to one of his favourite subjects, space.
▼

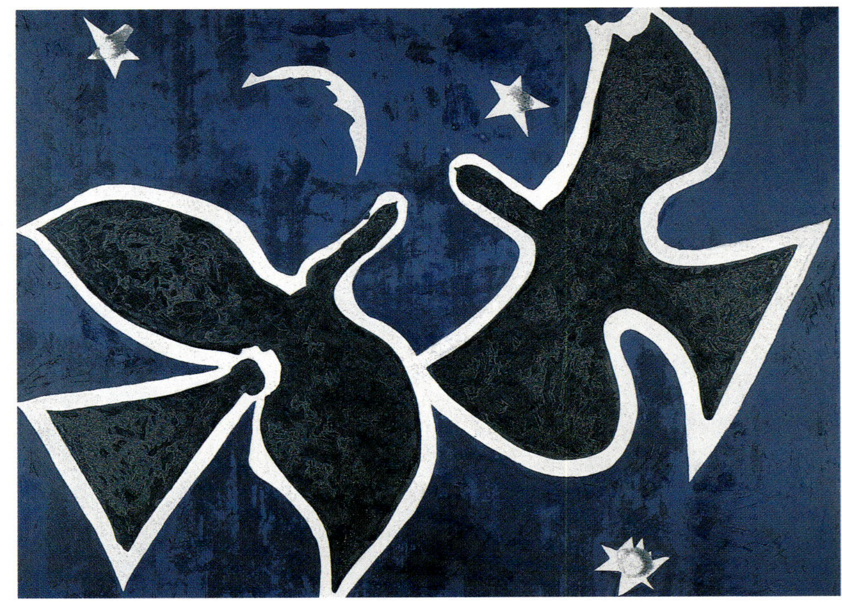

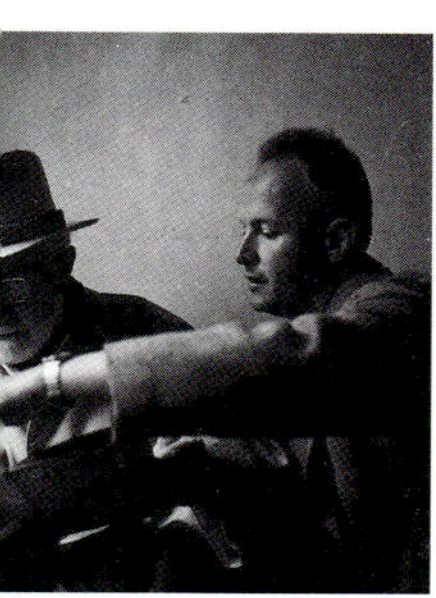

▲
Matisse and the photographer Cartier-Bresson at Tériade's house in Saint-Jean-Cap-Ferrat. Photograph taken in 1951. Musée Matisse collection, Nice.

In 1943 the publisher Tériade moved into the Villa Natacha in Saint-Jean-Cap-Ferrat. The house became a meeting place for painters, writers, sculptors and photographers.

Planes lead naturally to birds. Matisse decided to build a huge aviary in his studio: he could then watch the birds flying whenever he wanted. For him, cutting out paper shapes was a bit like flying. "I'd say that [the paper cut-outs] are a kind of graphic, linear equivalent of the feeling of flying", he told his friend André Verdet.

pasted paper is not collage!

Matisse had already used pasted paper. In *The Dance* he worked on the balance of form and colour by moving coloured cardboard shapes around. In 1937 he made models of set designs for *The strange farandole*, including one representing a black figure on a blue background.
The idea of sticking paper on to a picture was invented not by Matisse but by the Cubists. The first collage was by Picasso in 1912 (*Still-life with a Cane Chair*; Musée Picasso, Paris). Shortly afterwards Georges Braque stuck painted paper on his canvases. Between 1916 and 1929 the Dada movement used the idea in its mockery of everything, including itself. This was continued by Surrealism, led by the writer André Breton; collages and unlikely juxtapositions were used to express the world of the unconscious.

carving colour

Matisse's approach was different. He never used prefabricated material (coloured paper), which would introduce a "real" element into his picture. He went on simplifying, trying to get to the essential point: why draw an outline and colour it in when you could draw with scissors, directly in colour?

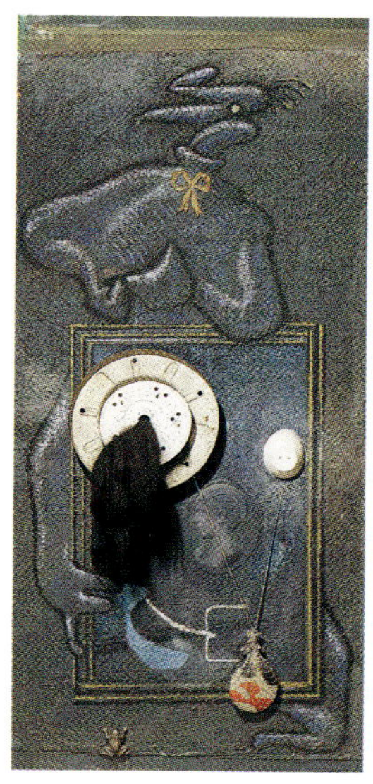

▲
Max Ernst (1891-1976), *Loplop Introduces a Girl* (1930-66). Oil on wood with various objects: 194 x 89 x 10 cm.

Max Ernst was a Surrealist. Between 1929 and 1934 he made a series of pictures featuring his emblem, Loplop the bird. By bringing together objects that have nothing in common, he was trying to touch the unconscious self and to express that which is beyond the scope of reason.

the story of an artist's book

"Icarus" was not a one-off cut-out. Between 1943 and 1947 Matisse made 20 of them for the illustrated book *Jazz*. Tériade, his publisher, was worried. How could these cut-outs be printed without spoiling the colours? By lithography? Impossible: the process changes the tones. The only solution was to transpose the plates to the "stencil" by using inks of the same brand as the gouaches used by Matisse. Their manufacturer was still in existence, but the necessary ingredients were unobtainable during the war because they came from Germany.
During the summer of 1946 the layout was finished and the format set. The book would comprise 146 pages, with 20 colour plates. It would be called *Jazz* and not *The Circus* as planned. Matisse wrote everything by hand, to "decorate" the pages: he said that his

The stencil
The outline of the drawing is cut out from a cardboard or metal plate. A sheet placed underneath is covered in colour with a brush. This technique is generally used to reproduce drawings on cloth or wall-paper. For *Jazz* the work was given to a talented colourist, Edmond Vairel.

Fernand Léger ▶
(1881-1955), *Two Tightrope Walkers* (1950). Lithograph for *The Circus*, Paris, Tériade, 1950. Photograph, Bibliothèque Nationale, Paris.

After the success of *Jazz*, Tériade asked Fernand Léger to write a book. Léger chose a completely different style from that of Matisse, but drew on the same theme, the circus.

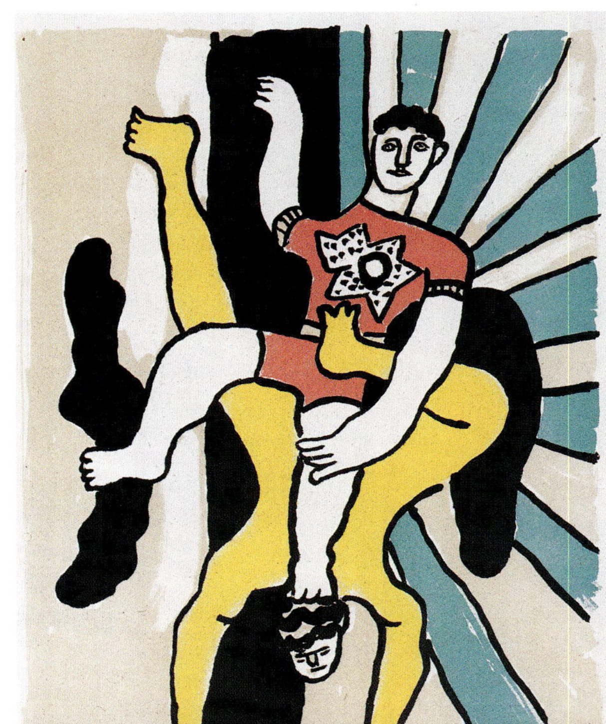

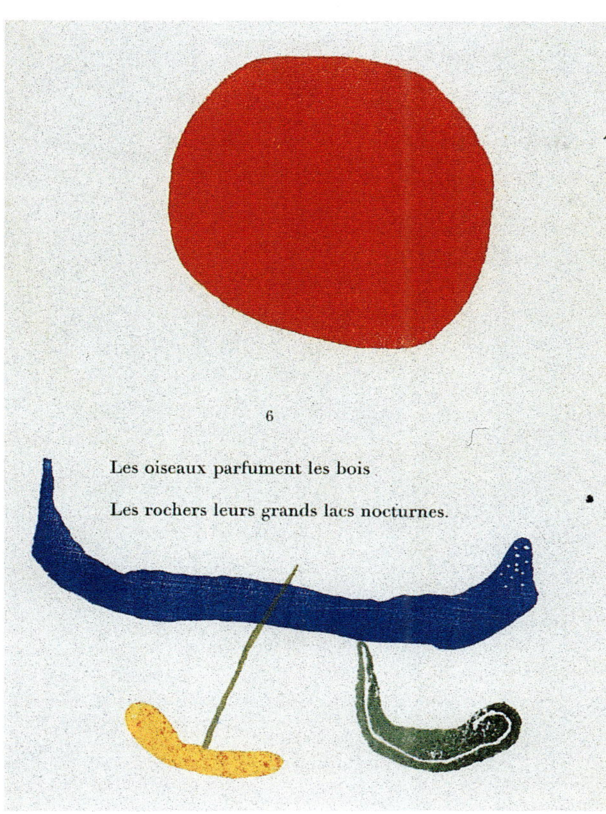

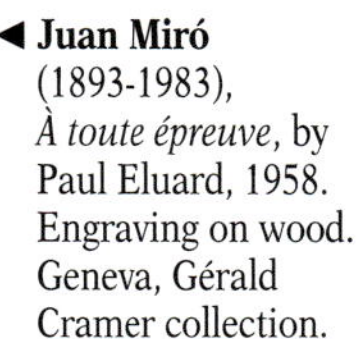

◄ **Juan Miró** (1893-1983), *À toute épreuve*, by Paul Eluard, 1958. Engraving on wood. Geneva, Gérald Cramer collection.

"To reach the maximum intensity with the minimum of means". This motto of Miró's was shared by Matisse.

No ordinary publisher
Tériade started as co-editor, with Skira, of the Surrealist magazine *Minotaur*. However he soon left. In 1937 he and his collaborator Angèle Lamotte set up a new art magazine called *Verve*. The greatest artists of the 20th century would contribute to it.

words were just "background sound" for his colours. The book is constructed like a piece of music through the relationship between black, white and colour, which Matisse called his "chromatic and rhythmic improvisations".

In September 1947 *Jazz* finally left Draeger, the printers. Matisse was disappointed by the stencil; where was the purity of the scissor-cut? But he acknowledged that the colours were faithful. If he could see the originals today he would be very surprised. The gouache colours have lost much of their brilliance. Those in the book, on the other hand, have remained unaltered.

Jazz was amazingly successful. People were talking about a "new departure" for Matisse. Matisse himself thought that with these cut-outs he had at last succeeded in synthesising his entire life's work.

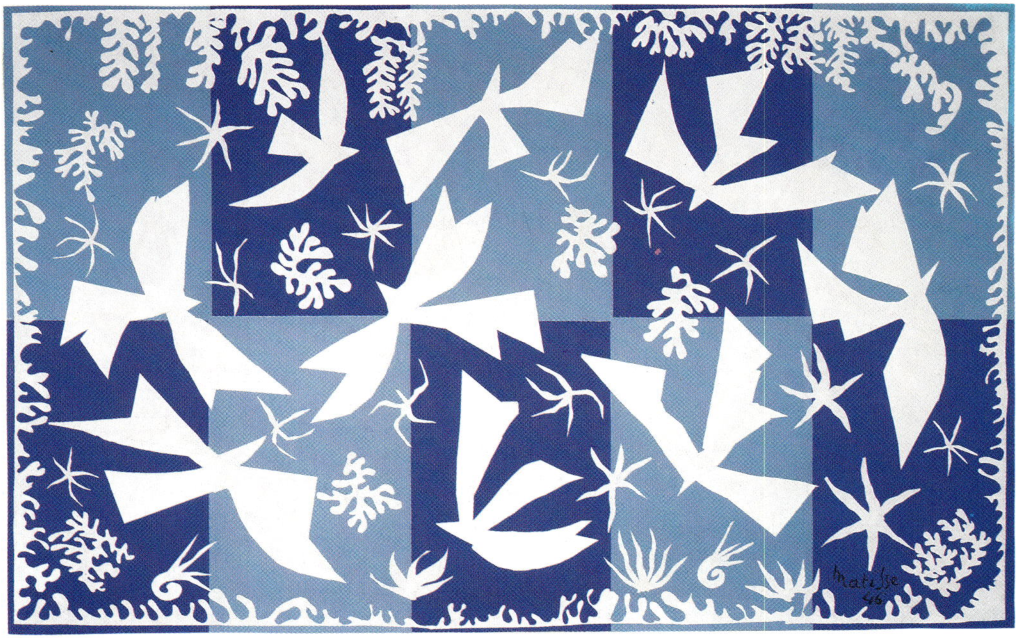

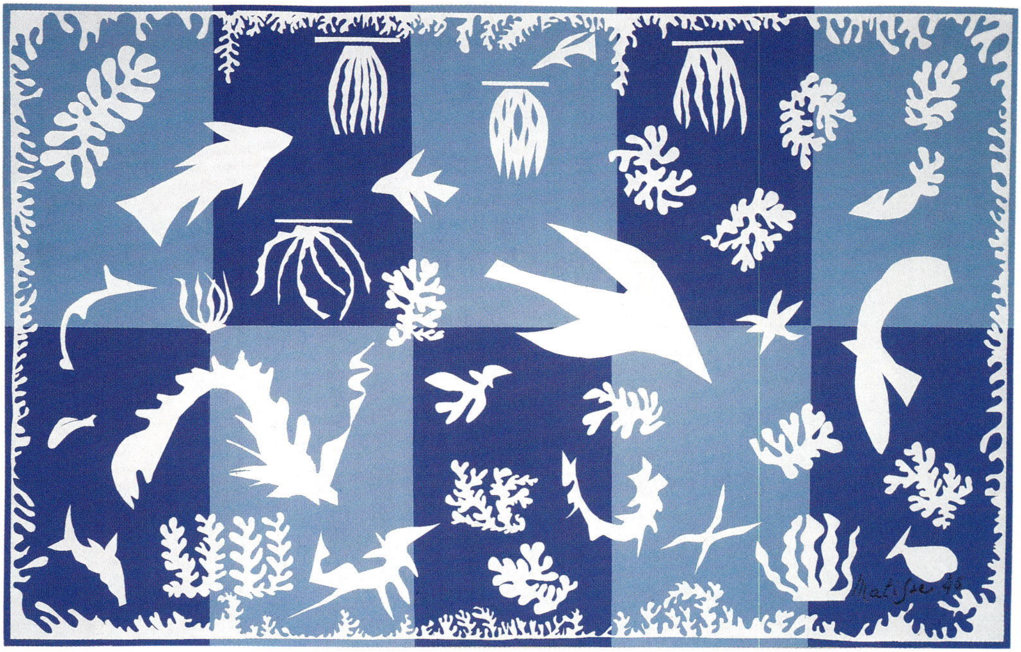

Matisse and drawing within painting

After *Jazz* Matisse continued to use paper cut-outs. He had perfected the process, but now he wanted to exploit all its possibilities. Though aged 78, he retained a fresh eye, which allowed him to keep renewing his artistic language until the very last moments of his life. His paintings, writings and many interviews show him to have been a lucid, sensitive, modest and indeed humble man. Nothing, he repeated, can ever be taken for granted; you always have to fight against the "easy pencil stroke". He dedicated his whole life to work, and his work to light.
Matisse spent over 60 years searching for one thing: the reconciliation of line with colour. He found a solution in 1941, with his paper cut-outs. Replacing pencil and brush with scissors was not only an ingenious idea but, above all, for Matisse it was the answer. Like a sculptor carving "into the quick of the colour", he had succeeded in linking line with colour and shape with surface.

◄ *Polynesia, the Sky* (1946).
Paper cut-outs retouched with gouache and glued on to canvas: 200 x 314 cm.

Polynesia, the Sea (1946).
Paper cut-outs retouched with gouache and glued on to canvas: 196 x 314 cm.

Inspired by his trip to Tahiti, these two panels are tapestry cartoons, destined for the Gobelins workshop. In a blue and white universe, seaweed touches the stars and birds swim with fish. But the horizon, marked by a few horizontal lines, appears only in the sea.

After covering sheets of white paper with gouache, Matisse would pin them up on his studio walls. The colours were so violent that a doctor advised him to wear sunglasses! Gradually the entire space was filled with his paper cut-outs. His studio itself became an immense canvas. He played with colours and shapes, moving his forms around until he found the best place for them. In 1946 he was visited by an English industrialist who asked him to paint some scarves. Stimulated by his love for fine materials,

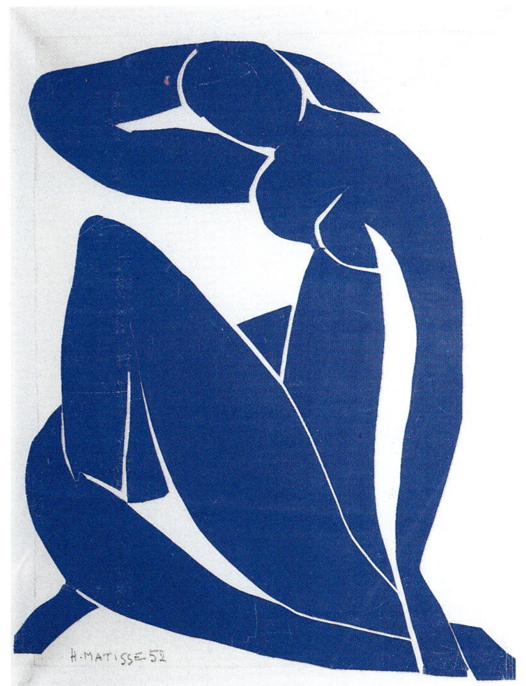

▲
Blue Nude II (1952).
Gouache on paper cut-outs, stuck on white paper glued to canvas: 116.2 x 88.9 cm.

Matisse made four *Blue Nudes*; two of these, *Blue Nudes II* and *III*, are in the Musée National d'Art Moderne in Paris. *Blue Nude I* is in a private collection and *Blue Nude IV* is in the Musée Matisse in Nice.

▶
Blue Nude III (1952).
Gouache on paper cut-outs, stuck on white paper glued to canvas: 112 x 73.5 cm.

Blue becomes a body, a woman's body becomes light. It is the gaps that give the bodies their shapes and set them in a space. This is drawing, painting and sculpture all at once.

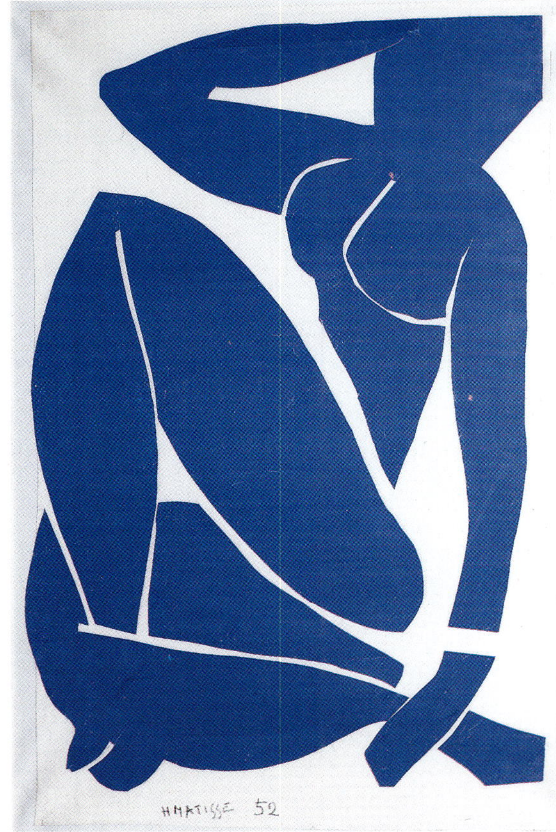

Matisse used the beige walls of his Paris apartment in Boulevard du Montparnasse to stick up his shapes cut from white paper. In this way he developed two panels, *Oceania, the Sky* and *Oceania, the Sea*. These were transferred to linen by serigraphy. They were followed by two other, similarly inspired panels: *Polynesia, the Sky* and *Polynesia, the Sea*. These were tapestry cartoons, designed to be woven by the Gobelins tapestry workshop. As early as 1935 he had made *Window in Tahiti*, a cartoon for the Beauvais workshop.

Why these exotic themes? Matisse went to Tahiti in 1930. His trip left deep traces, which resurfaced here. He chose to frame each series in the same way: waving edges that are by turns waves, seaweed, coral and leaves, conveying the existence of sea life at a deep level. He even painted birds in the sea, no doubt an allusion to Icarus and the emotions called up by his first flight in an aeroplane. But above all, he had found a new way of melting all spaces into one, the sea in the sky, as he had often done with the inside and outside of his studio.
Matisse completed other large compositions in the same spirit, such as *Sea Beasts* (1950, National Gallery of Art, Washington), *The Wave* (1952, Musée Matisse, Nice) and *The Swimming Pool* (1952, Museum of Modern Art, New York).

Although on a smaller scale, the *Blue Nudes* are no less monumental. It is not their real size that conveys a sense of immensity, but the space around them. Matisse gives them three dimensions without employing any optical illusions, using only the interplay of empty and full space. A single colour, blue, is enough to give them an expression of profundity and inner life. How does he manage, with so little, to touch the most secret things in human beings, their spiritual life?
"In art, truth, reality begins when you no longer know what you're doing."

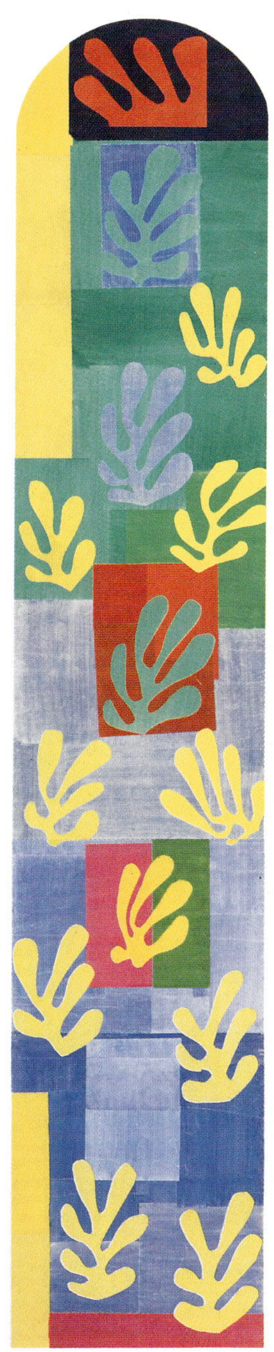

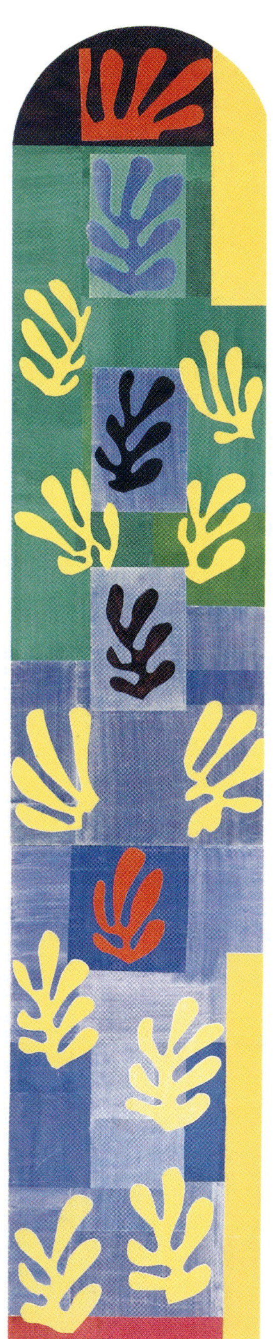

◀ *Design for the Pale Blue Window* (December 1948-January 1949). Gouache on paper cut-outs, stuck on brown paper, then on strong white paper. The whole (14 panels) is glued on canvas. 5.15 metres high, 2.52 metres wide (in two pieces).

PALE BLUE WINDOW

December 1948-January 1949

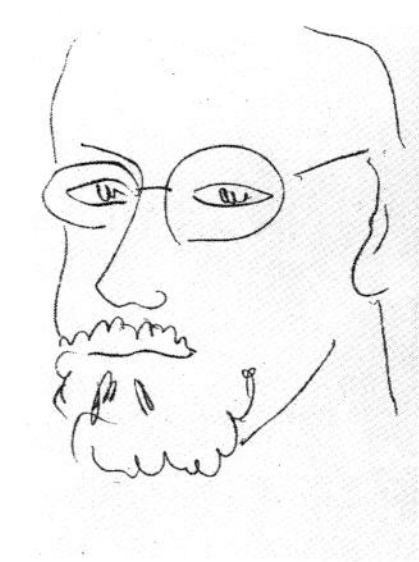

▲ *Three-quarters Self-portrait* (1948). Lithograph: 22.9 x 18.5 cm. Bibliothèque Nationale, Paris.

A design for a chapel window, a nun friend of the painter, and Matisse was off on a new adventure: creating the Chapelle du Rosaire in Vence.

Why are these forms "lobed"?
In the region around Nice there is a variety of cactus that Matisse had often drawn. According to the *Book of Revelations*, cactus flowers will heal the pagans. Matisse very logically used this as inspiration for his chapel, particularly since the cactus shape reminded him of the seaweed of Tahiti.

In the spring of 1947 Matisse came across Monique Bourgeois again, or rather Sister Jacques-Marie, as she had become. She had entered the convent in Vence and had come for some help: she wanted a new window for her chapel. On the painter's advice, she made a model in coloured paper, which Matisse revised. He soon became caught up in the idea.

a rainbow in a chapel

Lighting up a holy place – what a challenge for an artist who is always seeking light! His first model, inspired by the *Book of Revelations*, did not satisfy him. He made another, full-scale model in paper cut-outs. With his head full of visions of Tahiti, he invented a "pattern of forms" with leaves, flowers, seaweed and coral. The lobed shapes are mainly yellow, stuck on green and blue paper. This luminous yellow is answered by the more orangey yellow of the vertical strips in the corners. There are a few red shapes and strips of bright pink at the base. Matisse also uses effects of positive and negative: the green leaf on a blue background at the top left is answered by two blue leaves on a green background, below and right. Imagine the light pouring through this concert of pure colour.... If only the *Pale Blue Window* had been made!

a chapel like a big open book

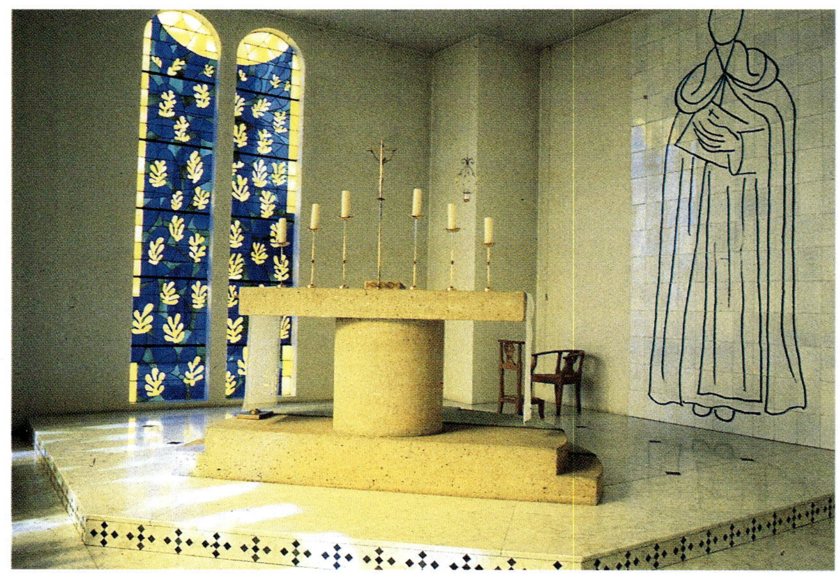

▲ Interior of the Chapelle du Rosaire, photograph.

On the left is the completed window representing the "Tree of Life" (design in the Vatican Museum, collection of Modern Religious Art); on the right is St Dominic.

Colour helps to express light, not as a physical phenomenon, but as the only light that really exists, that in the artist's mind. Matisse.

Matisse worked with two Dominican monks who loved modern art, Brother Rayssiguier on the architecture and Father Couturier on the window. Matisse showed Father Couturier the design for the *Pale Blue Window* in 1949, but ... disaster! He had forgotten the iron bars to hold the window in place. He had to start again, for the third and last time.
Should there be any red? Nothing is red in this chapel; and yet Matisse saw it. "It exists by contrast with the

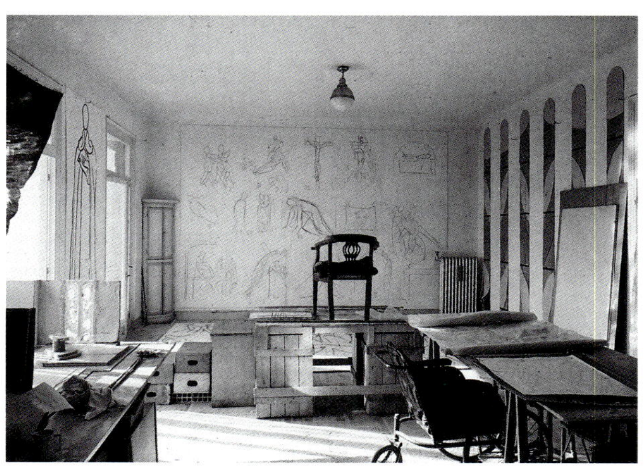

Matisse's apartment in the Hôtel Régina in Cimiez. ▶

So that he could work more easily on the chapel window, Matisse moved from his villa in Nice early in January 1949 back into his studio apartment at the Régina, which, by coincidence, was the same shape as the chapel.

◀ Matisse cutting out. Photograph.

"I cut these gouache paper cut-outs the way you would cut glass; only here they are often arranged to reflect light, whereas for the window they must be arranged so that light will pass through them." Matisse, to Brother Rayssiguier, when looking through *Jazz*.

Religion and art in the 20th century
During World War II Father Marie-Alain Couturier, who was himself an artist, opened the Institut Français d'Art Moderne at the Ecole des Hautes Etudes Françaises in New York. In 1948, three years after his return to France, he took up again the editorship of *L'Art sacré* ("Sacred art"), which he had set up in 1937. Through his efforts, the greatest French artists became involved in designing and decorating new churches. In 1950 Maurice Novarina built the church of Notre-Dame-de-Toute-Grâce on the Assy plateau in Haute-Savoie. Artists such as Lurçat, Bonnard, Léger, Rouault, Braque, Matisse and Chagall all worked on it. The church of the Sacré-Coeur in Audincourt (Doubs) has stained glass by Léger, Bazaine and Le Moal, a tapestry by Léger and a mosaic by Bazaine.

colours that are there. It exists by reaction, in the mind of the onlooker," he said.
Of all the colours in the *Pale Blue Window*, Matisse kept only three. On a lemon yellow background, flowers of the same yellow bloom among ultramarine and bottle green leaves. The window's refinement stems not from the quality of the colours, but from their quantity and harmony.

opposite the windows, black and white

Matisse did not confine himself to the windows. To achieve an overall effect he rethought the entire interior of the chapel. He wanted it white, pure and simple. On the walls opposite the windows he planned three sober and stylised decorations, black lines on white ceramics: St Dominic by the altar, the Virgin and Child in the nave and the Way of the Cross at the end.
Gradually Matisse made the designs for his chapel to be like a double page of a book. The left-hand page, the window, was all in colour. The right-hand page was white, on which were black lines like writing. As in *Jazz*, he was looking for a balance between colour and line.

I want all who enter my chapel to feel purified and eased of their burdens.

how to attain purity?

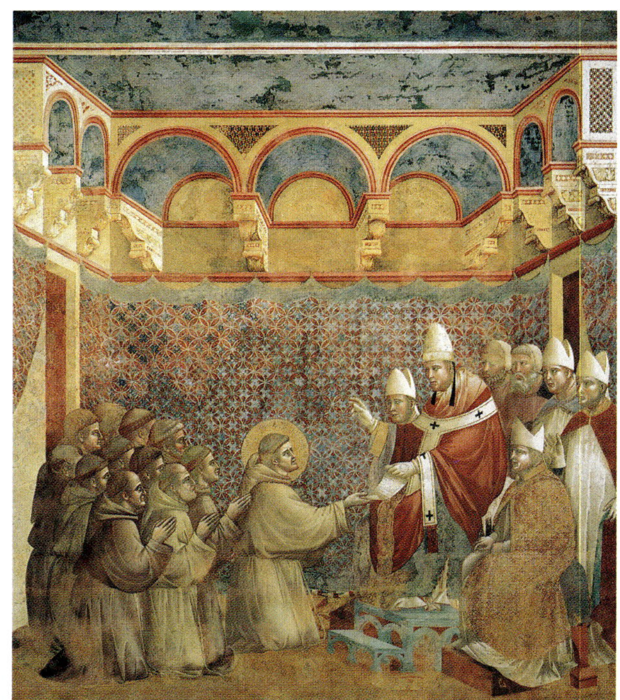

◀ **Giotto di Bondone** (1266-1377), *Approval of the Franciscan Rule by Pope Honorius III* (c. 1296-1304). Fresco, higher church of St Francis of Assisi.

"For me Giotto is the peak of my desires, but the road that leads to an equivalent in our time is too much for one life." Matisse, in a letter to Bonnard, 1946.

Stained glass
Matisse felt a great affinity with the art of the Middle Ages. When he visited Chartres Cathedral, he discovered the expressive power of stained glass. "In Chartres," he wrote, "stained glass is both colour and light; later they felt the need to vary the elements of the composition and to tell stories; at that point the essential spirit of stained glass was abandoned. Stained glass should have the expansiveness of organ music, without the need for words."

Matisse designed everything in the chapel – the furniture, the altar, the objects used in services, the chasubles, the chandeliers, the pediment over the entrance, a ceramic, a 13-metre wrought iron cross... Four years of work for a complete work of art.

Few artists in the 20th century worked for the Church. Georges Rouault is certainly the most important religious painter. Matisse always dreamed of an art of "balance, purity and tranquillity". He admired Giotto, the 14th-century Italian painter, for this very reason.

In an article published in *La Grande Revue* in 1908 he wrote: "When I see Giotto's frescos in Padua I don't worry about which scene from the life of Christ I am looking at; but at once I understand the feeling that it radiates, for it is in the lines, in the composition, in the colour, and the title will only confirm my impression."

According to Matisse, all art worthy of the name is religious. Every artist must reach the one essential thing, which is expressed in a single sign. This sign makes it possible to address all people of every religion. Matisse regarded the Chapelle du Rosaire as the "flower" of his entire work. In it he expressed his "essential thing", the colour-light that he finally found in himself. "When I enter the chapel," he wrote in March 1952, a year after it was consecrated, "I feel that my whole self is there – all that was best in me when I was a child, that I have tried to preserve throughout my life."

Each to his own chapel
"But why are you doing these things? I would approve if you were a believer. Since that's not the case, I think you do not have the moral right." This was the sharp reaction from Picasso. However, in 1952 he himself designed two large decorations, *War* and *Peace*, for a disused Gothic chapel in Vallauris. Today this chapel is a museum.

Marc Chagall ▶
(1887-1985),
Stained-glass window for Metz Cathedral (1959-60).

Of Matisse's contemporaries, Chagall was without doubt the most involved in church decoration. In 1956 he designed two grisaille windows for the church in Assy; two years later he repeated the experiment in Metz, introducing colour.

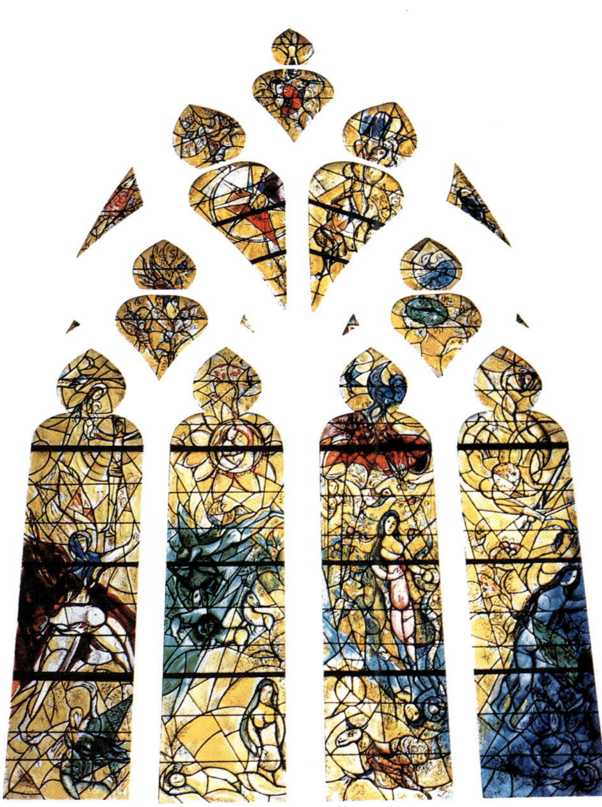

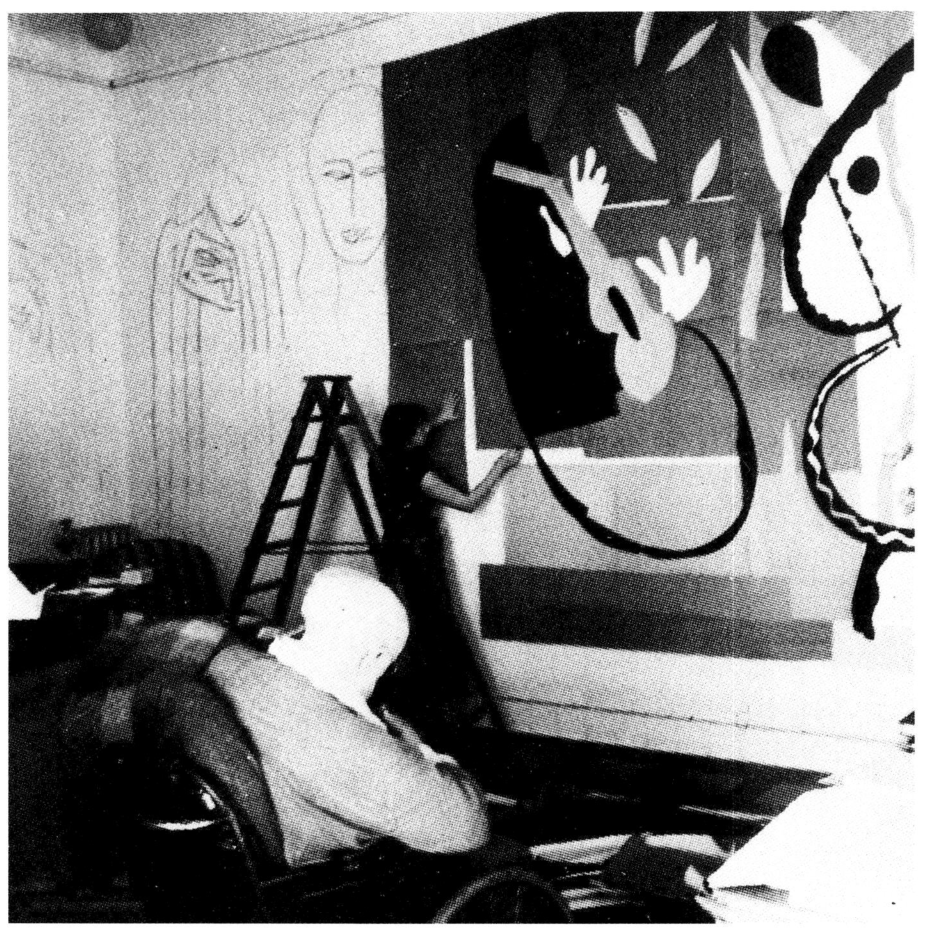

▲
Matisse in his studio in the Régina during work on *The Sorrow of the King*. Photograph taken early 1952.

The painter cut out the shapes and directed his assistant to position them on the wall with pins. In 1952 he made more than 40 gouache cut-outs in this way. They are of different sizes, and the smallest is not by any means the least important (the series of *Blue Nudes*, for example).

A step-by-step analysis

THE SORROW OF THE KING

1952

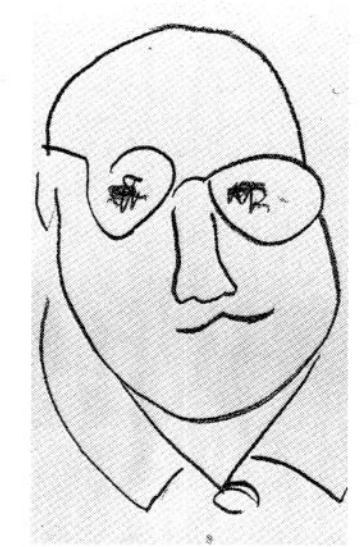

▲
Self-portrait (1951).
Lithograph:
31 x 21.2 cm.
Bibliothèque
Nationale, Paris.

Picasso and Aragon were worried about their friend Matisse; had he become definitively embroiled in religious art while working on his chapel? No! The painter of *The Joy of Living* had not yet said his last word.

In January 1949, when he left his villa Le Rêve ("The Dream"), Matisse moved back to the Hôtel Régina in Cimiez. The large studio was better suited to his work. After the designs for the Chapelle du Rosaire in Vence, he wanted to continue working on large gouache cut-outs.
The year of 1952 began with a commission for a stained-glass window from the American *Life* magazine. This became *Christmas Night* (in New York). It gave Matisse an opportunity to plunge once again into large decorative works, which appeared and reappeared on the walls of his apartment. The many photographs taken at the time reveal this process.
Most of the time he was working "in the dark"; his cut-outs were so large that he had to have them pinned straight on to the wall, without framing. Early in 1952 he started on a rather unusual work. On an enormous panel of nearly 12 square metres, he made a picture in gouache paper that is unique in his work in that it tells a melancholy story. In *The Sorrow of the King*, he speaks of old age, his old age. Aged 84, Matisse did a poignantly sad self-portrait, like many other painters do when they get old.

Have you seen a large panel at my place, in gouache with a figure: the sad king, a dancer with her charms and a figure scraping some kind of guitar, out of which flies a flock of gold-coloured flying saucers circling round the upper part of the composition and ending up around the moving dancer?
Matisse. Letter to Father Couturier, 8 May 1952.

The subject

Matisse probably drew on a book in the Bible. At first he had thought of illustrating the Song of Songs. He might also have chosen the scene painted by Rembrandt in 1657 in which the young David plays the harp to the old king Saul (the picture is in the Mauritshuis in The Hague). Or is this Salome, dancing for King Herod? Matisse very much liked the work of Gustave

The Sorrow of the King ►
(1952).
Gouache paper cut-outs, glued to canvas:
2.92 metres high,
3.86 metres wide.

Moreau, who painted two famous pictures of Salome in 1876: *The Apparition* (Musée Gustave Moreau, Paris) and *Salomé dancing* (The Louvre, Paris).
The story of Salome was very much in vogue in the late 19th century. The musicians Massenet and Strauss wrote two operas, *Hérodiade* (1881) and *Salomé* (1905); the writers Mallarmé, Flaubert, Laforgue and Oscar Wilde were inspired by it. In a poem called *La Vie antérieure* ("Former life") Baudelaire describes the sadness of a monarch lost in his memories.

The technique
Matisse "drew in colour" by using sheets of paper painted in gouache. Instead of a brush or pencil, he used scissors. He employed the technique of paper cut-outs periodically from the 1930s onwards (see *The Dancer*) and, with *Jazz*, gave it an independent status equal to that of painting.

The colours
The tones are "pure, light and brilliant" – in other words not three-dimensional. Matisse uses the contrasts and relationships between the colours:
– yellow gives different effects, depending on the background colour (blue, black, pink or green);
– the effect also depends on the surface colour (the king is black and white, the dancer white and black);

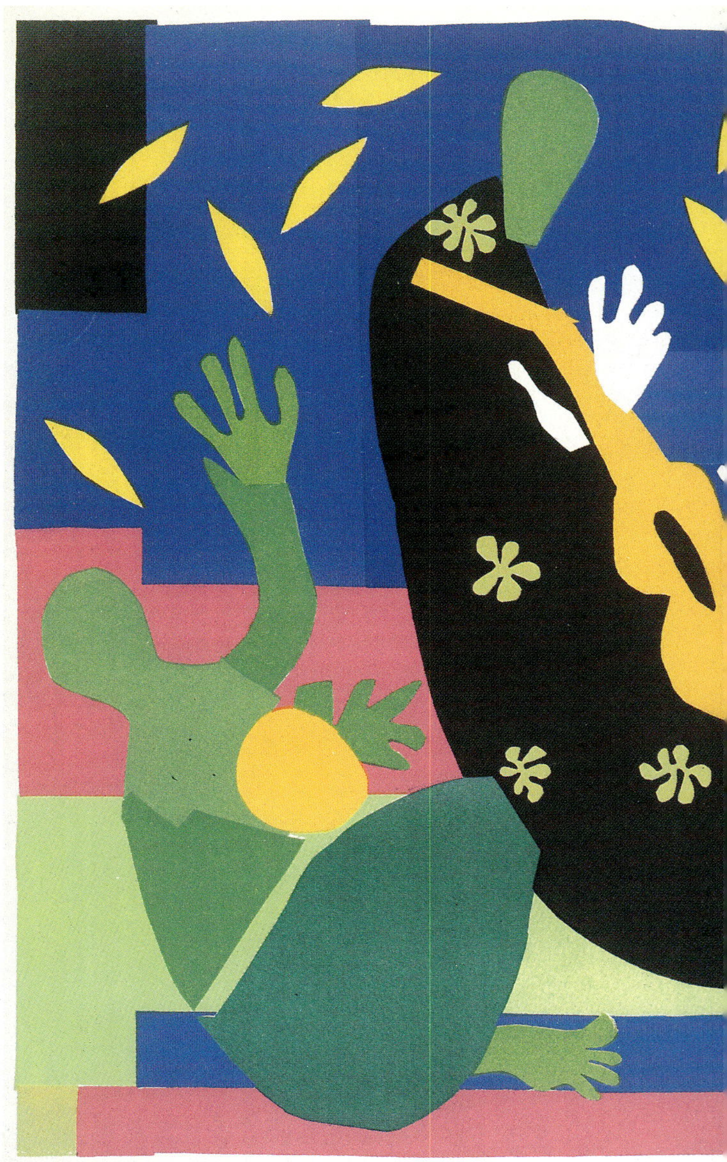

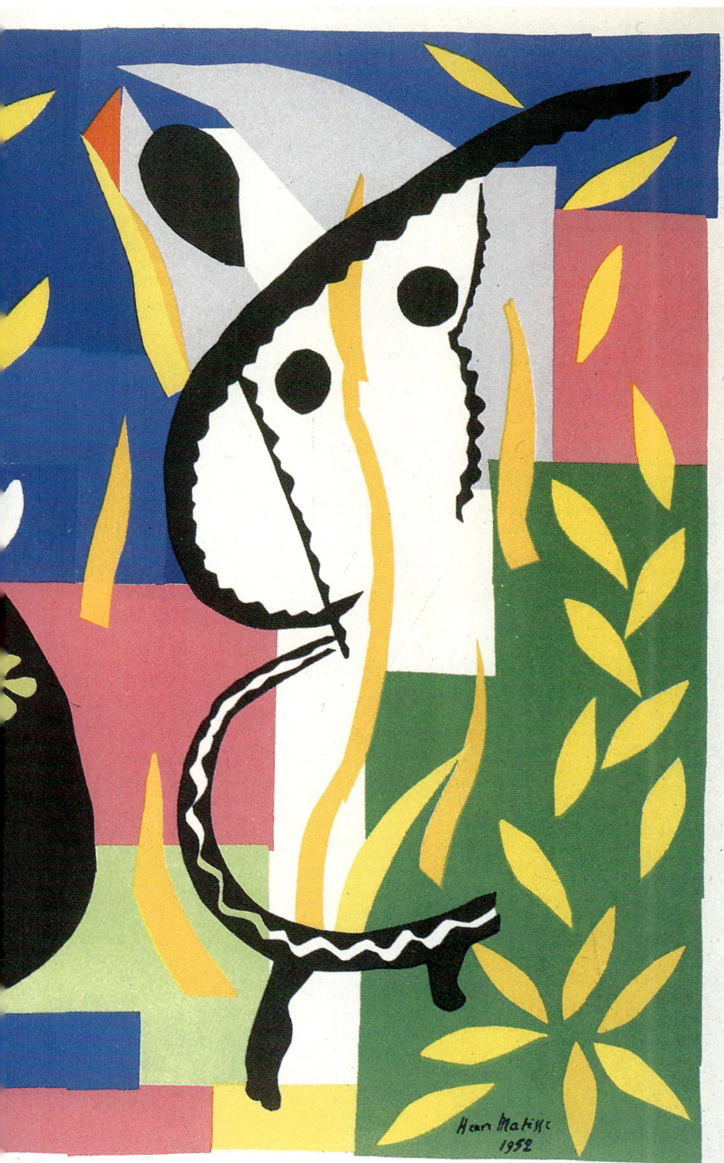

– real, "local", colours have disappeared. Matisse replaces the classic blue of the king's mantle with black. "You're not a slave to a blue", "black is a colour," said Matisse. The line is linked to the colour and the outline to the background:
– the dancer's white body is defined by the black cut-outs;
– the dance is created by linking two curves, held together by a white vertical shape which is the axis of the movement. "My curves are not crazy," said Matisse.

The design

All effects of illusion are absent, leaving the "sign" to speak:
– the faces are not detailed; expression is given by the overall shape (the bent head and body suggest the king's age and sorrow);
– the hands are like the flowers on the king's mantle: these lobed shapes (seaweed, coral, leaves, flowers) are signs of life;
– the figures' poses are rendered in purified forms, "distilled to the essential";
– the "golden flying saucers" allow Matisse to give rhythm to his composition. They are both musical notes and the Pacific light, which Matisse compared to "a deep golden goblet".
– in fact the musician (on the left) is a drummer. The guitar player is the king himself, in other words he is Matisse, alias the violinist at the window, surrounded by all he has loved music, dance, feminine beauty and light.

Biography

31 December 1869
Birth of Henri Matisse at Le Cateau-Cambrésis (Nord), son of Emile and Héloïse (née Gérard) Matisse. Spends his childhood in Bohain (Aisne). His parents are grain merchants.

1882-1887
Secondary school: the Lycée de Saint-Quentin.

1887-1888
Studies law at university in Paris; obtains his diploma in August 1888.

1889
Becomes a lawyer's clerk in Saint-Quentin.

1890
Convalescing from appendicitis, Matisse is "bitten by the demon painting".

1891-1892
Enrols at the Académie Julian (works in William Bouguereau's studio), then leaves to enter the École des Beaux-Arts and Gustave Moreau's studio. Fellow students include Simon Bussy, Albert Marquet, Georges Rouault, Henri-Charles Manguin, Charles Camoin, André Rouveyre, all of whom become his friends. Makes numerous copies of paintings at the Louvre.

1894
Birth of his daughter Marguerite.

1895
Moves to 19 Quai Saint-Michel. Trip to Britanny with Emile Wery.

1896
Shows four pictures at the exhibition of the Société Nationale des Beaux-Arts, of which he is made associate member; spends the summer at Belle-Ile with John Russell.

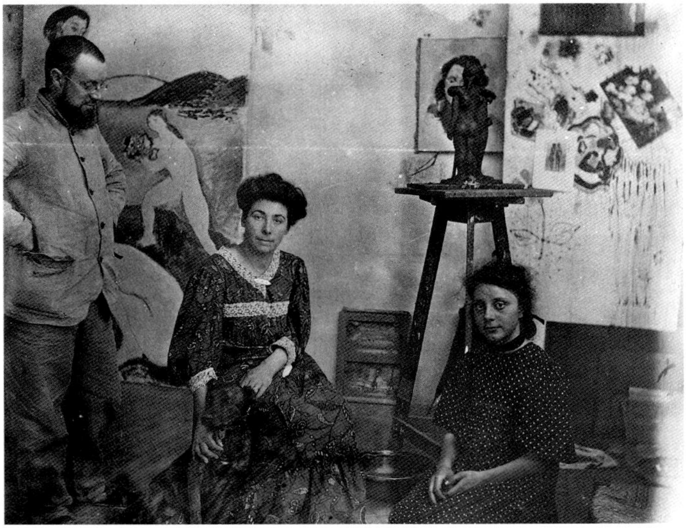

1897
Caillebotte legacy exhibited at the Musée du Luxembourg.

1898
Marries Amélie Parayre; honeymoon in London. Discovers the light of the Midi in Corsica, then Toulouse and around Perpignan.
♦ Death of Gustave Moreau.

1899
Returns to Paris after a year away. Birth of his son Jean. Begins to sculpt. Buys Cézanne's *Three Bathers*, a plaster-cast by Rodin, Gauguin's *Boy's Head*, a drawing by Van Gogh, all from Ambroise Vollard. Reads Signac's essay, "From Eugène Delacroix to Neo-Impressionism". Paints views of the Quai Saint-Michel. Meets painters André Derain and Jean Puy. Paints the *First Orange Still-life*.

1900
Birth of his second son, Pierre. In serious financial difficulties.

1903
Exhibits at the first Autumn Salon and at Berthe Weill's gallery. Completes his first engravings. Sculpts *The Slave*.
♦ Death of Gauguin. Marie Curie wins Nobel Prize for Physics.

1904
First one-man exhibition at Ambroise Vollard's gallery. Spends summer with Signac in Saint-Tropez. Starts to experiment with Divisionist technique. Shows 13

◄ 1907. Matisse in his studio with Amélie and Marguerite.

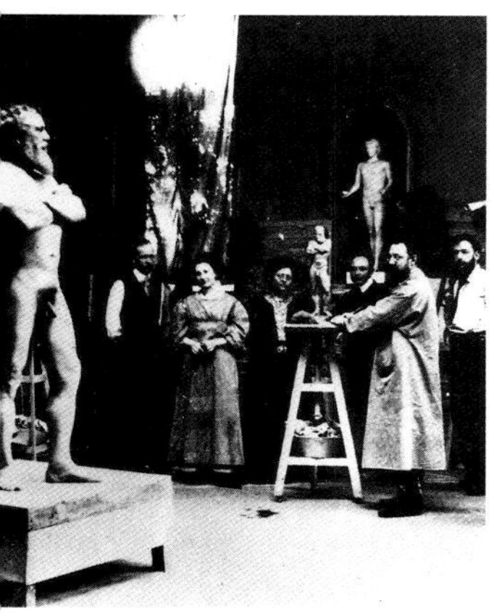

▲
1909. Matisse in the former Sacré-Cœur Convent (Hôtel Biron) with students from his painting academy.

pictures at the Autumn Salon. Paints *Luxe, calme et volupté* (bought by Signac in 1905 at the Salon des Indépendants).

1905
The Matisse family spend the summer in Collioure, with André Derain, meeting the sculptor Aristide Maillol and Daniel de Montfried. At the Autumn Salon Matisse appears as the leader of a group of painters derisively called "wild beasts" or "Fauves" (Friesz, Derain, Marquet, Manguin, Puy, Rouault, Valtat and Vlaminck). The Steins (Leo, Gertrude, Michael and Sarah) buy *Woman in a Hat*. Marcel Sembat buys his first Matisse.
♦ First Russian Revolution.
Albert Einstein's paper on relativity.

1906
Matisse exhibits *The Joy of Living* at the Salon des Indépendants, bought by Leo Stein. Exhibits at Druet's gallery. Trip to Algeria (Biskra), bringing back cloth and ceramics. Stays at Collioure, exhibits at the Autumn Salon. Matisse makes his first lithographs and becomes interested in African art.
♦ Cézanne dies.

1907
Matisse meets Picasso at the Steins', Rue de Fleurus (Paris). Trip to Italy (Padua, Florence, Arezzo and Siena). Paints *Le luxe I*. Paints and exhibits *Blue Nude* at the Salon des Indépendants. Matisse's admirers organise an academy in the former Des Oiseaux convent (Rue de Sèvres, Paris), where he teaches.

1908
Moves his studio into the former Sacré-Cœur convent, Hôtel Biron (Boulevard des Invalides, Paris). First exhibition of drawings in New York (arranged by the photographer Steichen) in Gallery 291, belonging to Alfred Stieglitz. Exhibits in London, Stockholm and Berlin. Trip to Bavaria with Hans Purrmann. Publishes *Notes d'un peintre*. Sergey Shchukin buys his *Red Table*.

1909
Shchukin commissions two decorative panels: *Dance* and *Music*. Matisse moves to Issy-les-Moulineaux, where he has a studio built. Sculpts *Serpentine* and *The Back I*.
♦ Louis Blériot crosses the English Channel in an aeroplane.

1910
Major Matisse exhibition at the Bernheim-Jeune gallery (Paris). Matisse goes to Munich with Marquet to see the exhibition of Near Eastern art. Trip to Spain.
♦ Chinese Revolution.

1912
Matisse, Camoin and Marquet in Morocco (Tangiers) until spring. First exhibition of Matisse's sculpture in New York. Returns to Tangiers in December.
♦ Balkans War.
Titanic sinks.

1912. Matisse dressed as a bedouin in Tangiers. ►

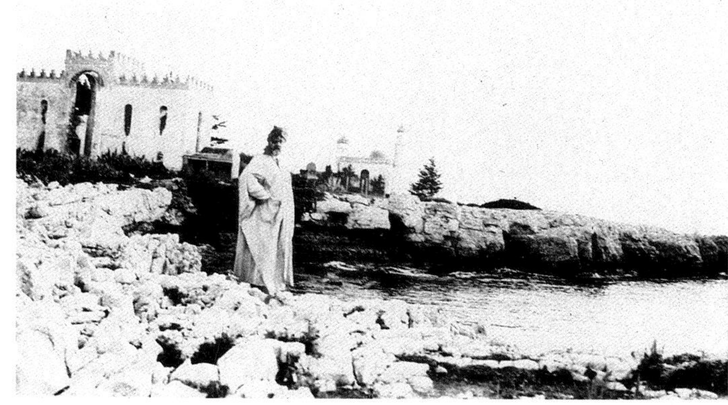

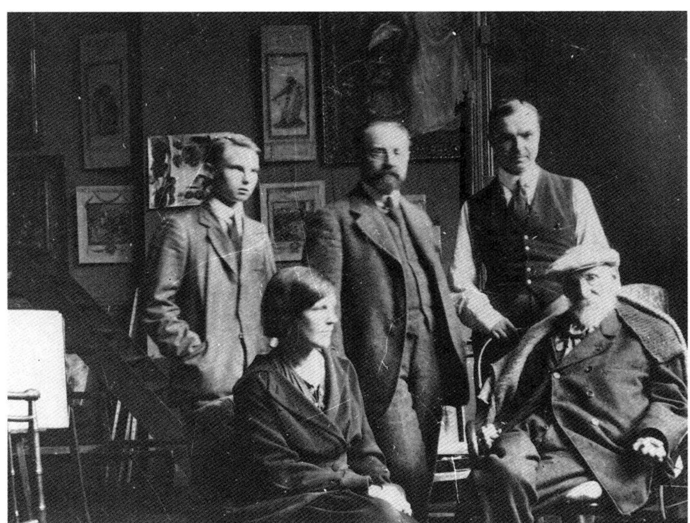

▲
1918. Matisse at Renoir's villa, Les Collettes, in Cagnes-sur-mer. Left to right: Claude Renoir, Greta Prozor, Matisse, Pierre Renoir, Auguste Renoir.

1913
Several of Matisse's works shown at the Armory Show, New York and then Chicago. Also participates in the Secession exhibition in Berlin. The Russian collector Morosov buys *Moroccan Triptych*. Matisse takes a studio at 19 Quai Saint-Michel (one floor below the old one). Sculpts *The Back II*.
♦ Second Balkans War.
Marcel Proust publishes *À la recherche du temps perdu* ("Remembrance of things past").

1914
Matisse works in Paris and Issy-les-Moulineaux. Exempted from military service. Spends the summer with his family at Collioure, where he meets the Cubist painter Juan Gris. Two Danish collectors, Tetzen Lund and Johannes Rump, start buying his pictures.
♦ World War I breaks out.

1915
Exhibition in New York, Montross Gallery. Spends the winter at Quai Saint-Michel.

1916
Works on *The Painter and his Model* in Paris and *The Piano Lesson* and *Still-life after de Heem* at Issy. First stay in Nice, at Hôtel Beaurivage. Exhibition in London.
♦ Battle of Verdun.
Birth of Dadaist movement in Zurich (Switzerland).

1917
Summer in Issy-les-Moulineaux (*The Music Lesson*) and autumn in Paris. In December leaves for Marseilles, then Nice (Hôtel Beaurivage). First visit to Renoir at Cagnes-sur-mer.
Sculpts *The Back III*.
♦ The USA enters the war. October Revolution in Russia. Rodin dies.

1918
Matisse-Picasso exhibition at Bernheim-Jeune gallery (Paris). Matisse first rents a studio near Hôtel Beaurivage, Quai du Midi, in Nice; paints *The Violinist at the Window* and a *Self-portrait*. Then moves to the Villa des Alliés; paints *Interior with Violin*. Spends the summer in Cherbourg and Paris. Returns to Nice, moves to Hôtel de la Méditerranée.
♦ 11 November: Armistice.
Shchukin and Morosov's collections confiscated by the new Soviet government.
Tsar and his family executed.

1919
In the spring Matisse exhibits at the Bernheim-Jeune gallery (Paris). In the autumn, a large exhibition at the Leicester Galleries (London).
♦ Treaty of Versailles signed.
Renoir dies.
Foundation of the Bauhaus, a teaching institution for the arts, Weimar, Germany.

1920
Designs sets for *Le rossignol* ("The song of the nightingale") for Diaghilev's Ballets Russes to music by Stravinsky; becomes friends with Leonid Massine. Goes to London to see the first night at Covent Garden. Spends summer in Étretat; paints 31 pictures there, which he then exhibits at Bernheim-Jeune's. Henriette Darricarrère poses for him (until 1929).

1921
Matisse spends summer in Étretat again. In autumn, rents a flat at 1 Place Charles-Félix in Nice. Musée du Luxembourg (Paris) buys *The Odalisque in Red Trousers*.

1922
Amélie and Marguerite donate *Interior with Aubergines* (painted 1911) to the Musée de Grenoble.
♦ James Joyce publishes *Ulysses*.

1923
Marcel Sembat leaves his Matisse collection to the Musée de Grenoble. The Shchukin and Morosov collections form the new Museum of Modern Western Art in Moscow.
♦ Hitler's failed putsch in Germany.

1924
In Copenhagen (Denmark) Leo Swane organises the biggest Matisse retrospective to date.
♦ André Breton publishes Surrealist Manifesto.

1925
Trip to Italy. Matisse paints *Decorative Figure in an Ornamental Background*. Sculpts a *Large Seated Nude*.

1927
Pierre Matisse organises an exhibition of his father's work at the Dudensing Gallery in New York. Henri wins Carnegie Prize. Paints *Reclining Nude* and *Odalisque in Grey Trousers*. Sculpts *Reclining Nude II*.
♦ Civil war in China.
Charles Lindbergh flies across Atlantic.
Juan Gris dies.
Birth of Mickey Mouse.

1930
Finishes *The Back IV*. Leaves for Tahiti, via New York and San Francisco. Visits Etta Cone in Baltimore and the Barnes Foundation in Merion. The publisher Skira commissions illustrations for Mallarmé's *Poésies*. Exhibits at the Tannhauser Gallery in Berlin. Second trip to New York. Is one of the judges for the Carnegie Prize, which is given to Picasso. Receives commission to make large decoration for the Barnes Foundation. Third trip, in December, to look at the site.
♦ 107 Nazi members of the Reichstag in Germany.

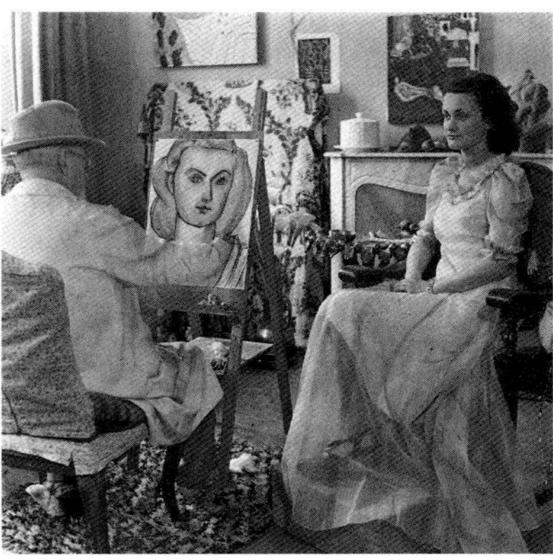

▲ 1946. Matisse painting Mme Lucienne Bernard, friend of the poet René Char.

Ghandi arrested in India.
André Malraux publishes *La Voie royale* ("The royal road").

1931
Several retrospectives in Paris, Basel and New York. Works on *The Dance* for the Barnes Foundation. In the autumn Pierre Matisse opens his own gallery in New York.

1932
Finishes the second version of *The Dance*. Starts on the third, with the right measurements. Publication of Mallarmé's *Poésies* with 30 etchings by Matisse.

1933
Goes to Merion to supervise the installation of the final version of *The Dance*. Then goes to rest in Italy. Sees Giotto's frescos in Padua again.
♦ Hitler becomes Chancellor of the

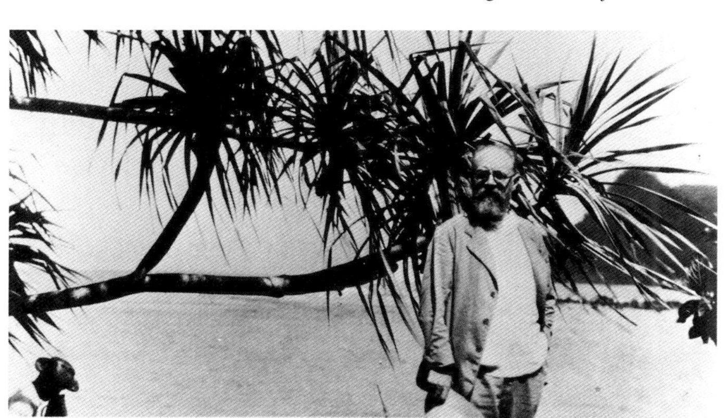

◀ 1930. Matisse in Tahiti in the spring. Photo F.W. Murnau.

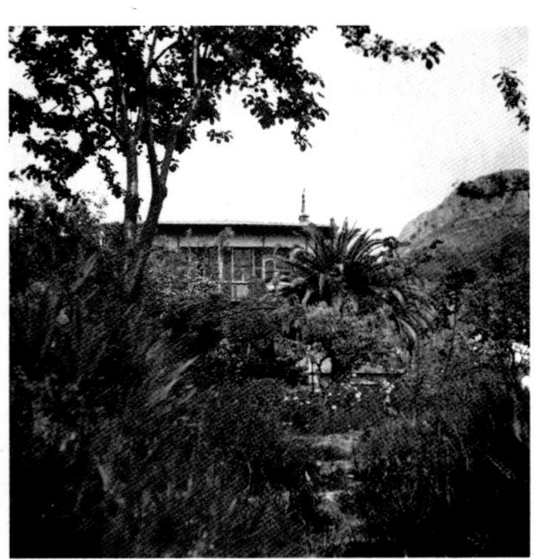

▲
1943-49. Villa "Le Rêve" in Vence.

Reich. First anti-semitic measures. The Joliot-Curies produce radioactivity artificially. Malraux publishes *La condition humaine* ("Man's estate"). Frederico Garcia Lorca publishes *Blood Wedding*.

1935
Year of intense work for Matisse. Lydia Delektorskaya poses for him: *Blue Eyes, The Dream, Pink Nude*. Matisse illustrates *Ulysses* by James Joyce, published in the USA.
♦ Hitler criticises modern art at the Nuremberg rally.
Gershwin composes *Porgy and Bess*.

1937
Exhibits recent paintings at the Paul Rosenberg gallery. Massine commissions sets and costumes for *The strange farandole* (or *Red and black*) for Ballets Russes. Matisse uses paper cut-outs for the models. *The Dance II* is bought by the Musée d'Art Moderne (Paris).
♦ Persecution of so-called "degenerate" artists in Germany.
Composer Maurice Ravel dies. Jean Renoir, son of the painter Auguste Renoir, makes the film *La grande illusion*.

1938
Matisse moves to the former Hôtel Régina in Cimiez. The state buys *Decorative Figure on an Ornamental Background.*

1939
The strange farandole opens in Monte Carlo. Spring in Nice, summer in Paris at the Hôtel Lutétia. In Geneva visits exhibition of pictures from the Prado.
♦ Poland invaded by German troops. War declared between Allies and Nazi Germany.
End of Spanish Civil War.

1940
When France is defeated, Matisse thinks of going to Brazil, but decides not to and returns to Nice in October: paints *The Romanian Blouse*.
♦ Franco-German armistice signed. Petain becomes French head of state.

1941
In January Matisse has an operation for intestinal cancer in Lyon, from which he recovers. Returns to Nice in May, starts painting again, in bed. First sketches for illustrations to *Le Florilège des amours* ("The anthology of love") by Ronsard.
♦ Germany attacks USSR. Japan attacks Pearl Harbour. The USA enters war.

1942
Writer Louis Aragon visits Matisse in Cimiez. Matisse reworks the series *Thèmes et variations* ("Themes and variations"), illustrates Charles d'Orléans' *Poèmes*. Cared for by a young nurse, Monique Bourgeois.

1943
Following an air-raid on Nice, moves to the villa Le Rêve ("The Dream") in Vence. Starts working on gouache cut-outs for his book *Jazz*. Monique Bourgeois becomes his model and assistant.
♦ Germans surrender at Stalingrad.
Jean-Paul Sartre publishes *L'Être et le néant* ("Being and nothingness"). The Expressionist painter Soutine dies.

1944
Amélie Matisse is imprisoned and Marguerite (married to Georges Duthuit) is deported for acts of resistance.
Matisse works on illustrations for *Les Fleurs du mal* ("The flowers of evil") by Baudelaire.
♦Paris liberated.
Kandisky, Munch and Maillol die.
Jean-Paul Sartre publishes *Huis-clos* ("In camera").

1945
Returns to Paris in the summer. Matisse-Picasso exhibition at Victoria & Albert Museum, London. Major retrospective of Matisse's work at the Autumn Salon, Paris. Exhibition of 13 pictures with photographs taken during their production at the Maeght Gallery.
♦ Germany surrenders.
Atomic bombs dropped on Hiroshima and Nagasaki.
Yalta and Potsdam conferences.

1946
Begins studies for the Chapelle du Rosaire in Vence (works on it constantly until 1950). Film by Campaux shows Matisse talking and drawing. He illustrates the *Lettres d'une religieuse portugaise.*
♦ Nuremberg trials.
Jackson Pollock does his first "action painting".

1947
Georges Salles and Jean Cassou (curators) acquire important works by Matisse for the newly created Musée National d'Art Moderne. Tériade publishes Matisse's "paint manuscript", *Jazz*. Matisse paints *Interiors* series in Vence.
♦ USSR breaks with the West.
Indian independence.
Bonnard dies.
André Gide wins the Nobel Prize for Literature.
Albert Camus publishes *La peste* ("The plague").

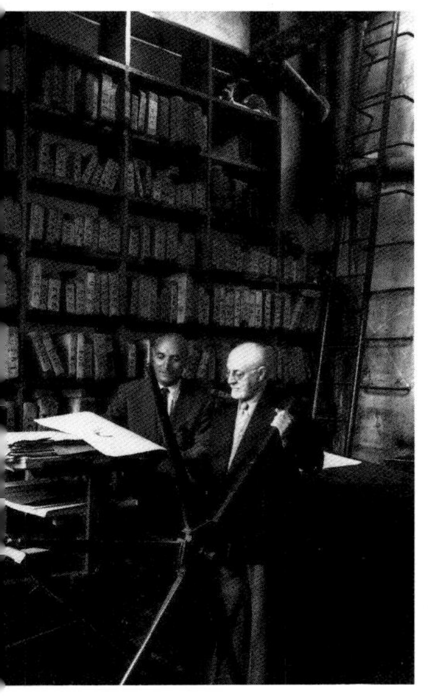

◀ Matisse and Fernand Moulot in the Mourlot brothers' studio.

1948
Matisse contributes a St Dominic to the decoration of the church at Assy. Henry Clifford organises Matisse retrospective in Philadelphia (USA). Matisse paints *Large Red Interior, The Pineapple, Interior with Egyptian Curtain.*
♦ Communists take over by force in Czechoslovakia.
Ghandi assassinated (India).
Declaration of state of Israel.
Start of Cold War.
Birth of the "Cobra", a European movement aiming to revive Expressionism.

1949
Matisse moves from Vence to the Hôtel Régina in Cimiez. Major exhibitions at Musée Nationale d'Art Moderne (gouache cut-outs) and at Lucerne (308 works shown). Baltimore Museum of Art acquires Cone collection.
♦ People's Republic of China declared.
Federal Republic of Germany created.
Composer Richard Strauss dies.
Simone de Beauvoir writes *Le deuxième sexe* ("The second sex").
Jean Cocteau films *Orphée.*

1950
Charles d'Orléans' *Poèmes* published with lithographs by Matisse. Exhibits at 25th Venice Biennale and wins the Grand Prize.

1951
25 June, Chapelle du Rosaire in Vence consecrated. Matisse returns to painting for the first time since 1948. Makes gouache cut-outs.

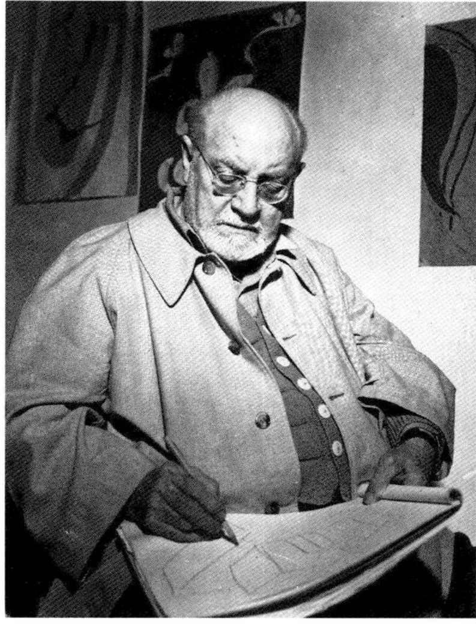

▲
Matisse designing the Chapelle du Rosaire. About 1950.

Matisse exhibition at National Museum in Tokyo.

1952
Very productive year for gouache cut-outs (over 40, including series of 4 *Blue Nudes*). Musée Matisse opened in Nice. Exhibition of engravings at the Berggruen gallery (Paris).

1953
Exhibition of paper cut-outs at Berggruen gallery.

1954
Exhibition at Paul Rosenberg Gallery in New York. Finishes his very last work, a gouache cut-out for the window of the Union Church of Pocantico Hills in New York.

3 November 1954
Henri Matisse dies in Nice. He is buried in the Cimiez cemetery.

Matisse seen by his friends

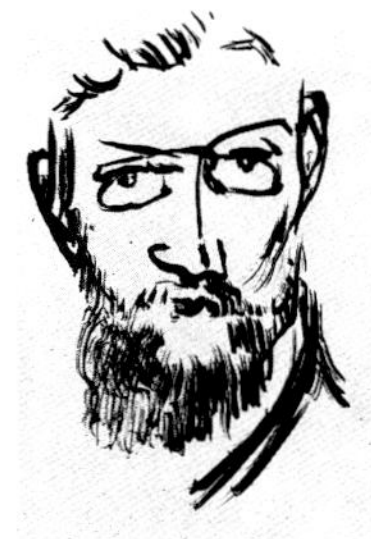

Picasso

"No painter has tickled painting into such bursts of laughter as Matisse."
Note on the back of a drawing, December 1951.

"A little Matisse, 3.2.71"
Note on the back of a drawing, 1971.

"There are certain things I can't talk about with anyone since the death of Matisse."

"All things considered, there's only Matisse."
Françoise Gilot, *Matisse et Picasso*.

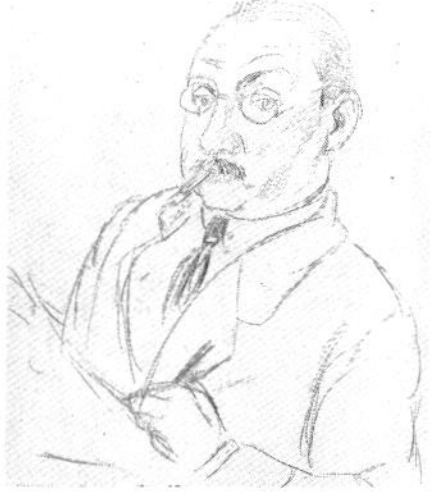

Louis Aragon

"Henri Matisse, man of the interrupted dream, need only be left alone for the simplest things, ordinary materials, to turn, in his hands, into objects of luxury, luxury itself."
Henri Matisse, a novel.

All arrangements of hair, in my hands, are undone.
The day has the colours that my hands give it.
Everything swollen by a sigh, in my room, sails
And the lasting dream is my gaze tomorrow.
[...]
I pay light its just tribute,
Immobile among the misfortunes of this time
I paint the eye's hope, so that Henri Matisse
May reveal to the future what humanity expects of it.
Novel

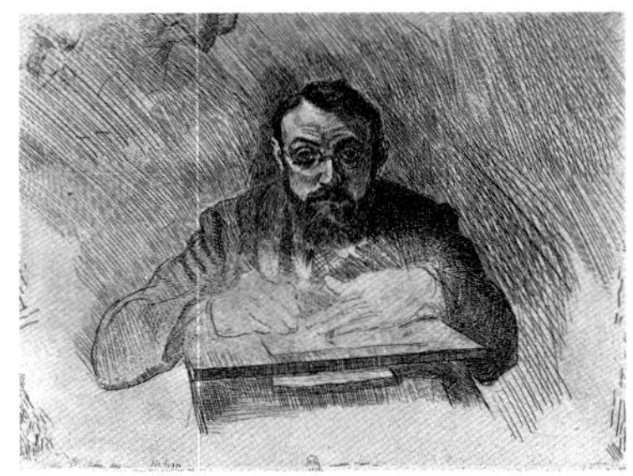

André Verdet

"Matisse's art shines and its gold is flesh and mind."

"Matisse's women.... They're enveloped in the fine desire that does honour."

"To live for a moment in Matisse's eye and look at the light. Perhaps we will emerge dazzled for a long time. Or blind forever.
"Matisse's eyes have been through dazzlement and triumphed over it.
"Light is all one, total, radiant, glorious. In its meaningful beauty and its victory, it has come close to the gulfs of the night."

"With Matisse, work is resplendent. It is the twin brother of holidays."

"I salute you, Henri Matisse, because you have saluted the existence and peace of things on earth."
Prestiges de Matisse, 1952.

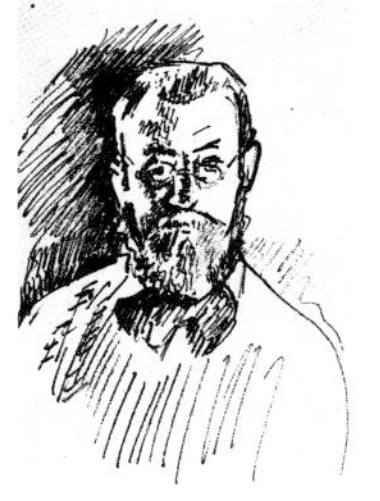

Pierre Bonnard

My dear Matisse,

I am glad that my research is appreciated by you. When I think of you, I think of a mind cleansed of all old aesthetic conventions; it is this alone that allows a direct view of nature, the greatest happiness a painter can have.
It's in part thanks to you that I can take advantage of it.
See you soon I hope.
Letter, January 1940.

Marcellin Pleynet

"Ultimately he seems the least 'scandalous' painter, in this concept of art the one who seems the closest (but also the most thoughtful) of that generation."
Teaching painting, 1970.

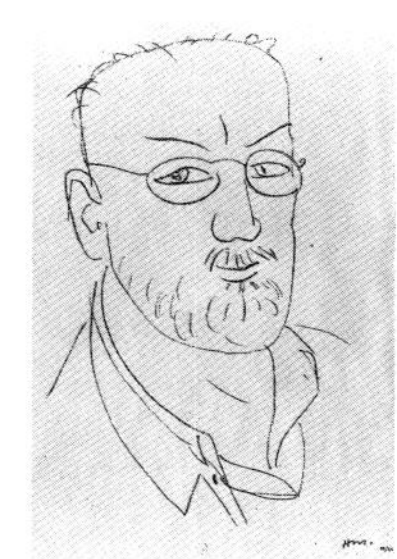

Guillaume Apollinaire

"If Henri Matisse's work is to be compared to anything, it would have to be an orange. Like an orange, Henri Matisse's work is a fruit of brilliant light."
Preface to the Matisse-Picasso catalogue.
Galerie P. Guillaume, Paris 1918.

Pierre Schneider

"In Matisse's subjective abstraction there is a trace of objective reality, a 'root' of reality that surfaces and changes everything. It is painting that remembers."
Le Figaro, 27 October 1992.

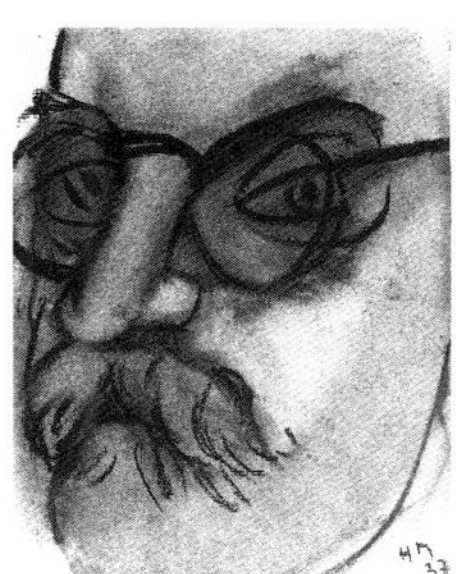

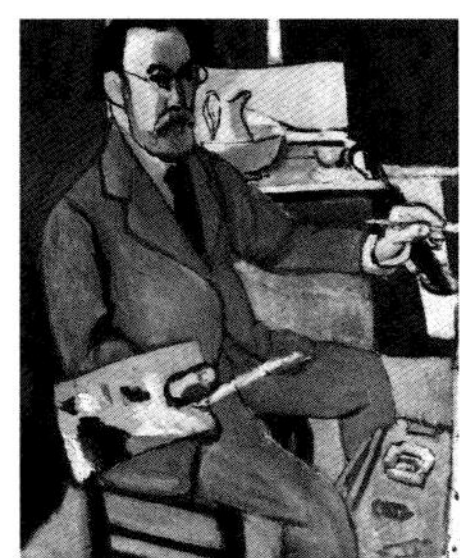

Brassaï

"In the light, bright studio, dressed in his white smock, Matisse looked like a hospital consultant. Curiously he already had that air when he was very young; his fellow students at the École des Beaux-Arts nicknamed him 'the doctor'. Matisse was irritated by his own starchyness. He often told me later, 'I'm a cheerful man, Brassaï, joyful even. But I'm taken for a serious-minded professor, I look like an old fogey'. And it was true. His severe appearance did not reflect his character. Matisse was a jolly fellow, ironic and curious."
Les Artistes de ma vie, 1982.

Christian Bobin

"In the evening of his life, Matisse painted with scissors. He cut storms of pure wine and springs of blue silk from the sky.
"He returned to the simple magic of colouring crayons. Day after day he gathered calm hours, like a child counts its joys one by one before falling asleep."
The Eighth Day of the Week.

André Masson

"It was very hard for him, very difficult. He used to criticise himself so strongly and so accurately too, putting his finger on what was wrong with his work.... The Matisse oasis, I'll never forget it!"
Interview with Georges Charbonnier, 1933.

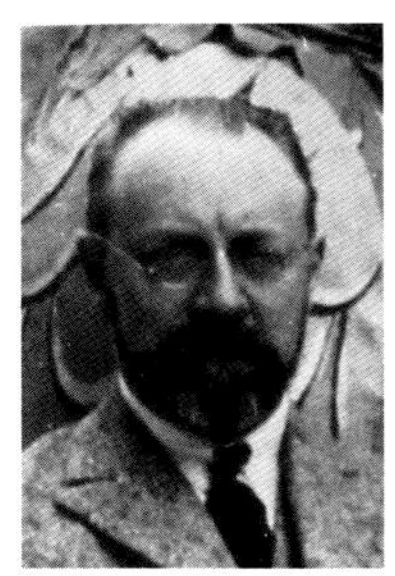

Pierre Reverdy

"You could doubtless say of him that he is not only the greatest colourist of his time, but the greatest optimist in French painting of all time. He grinds pink and blue as others do bitter colours, his pictures put sky in our eyes the way some large shells bring to our ears the quiet, distant rumble of the sea's waves."
"Matisse dans la lumière et le bonheur",
Verve, 1958.

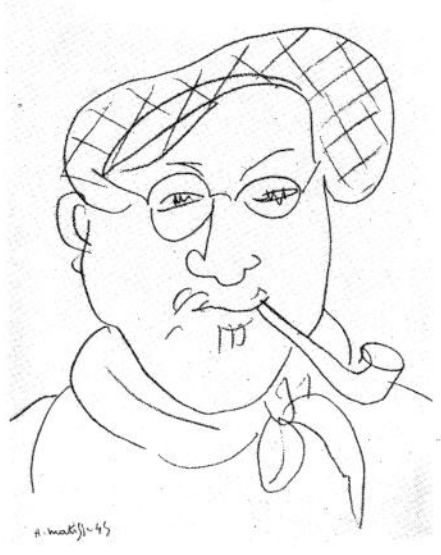

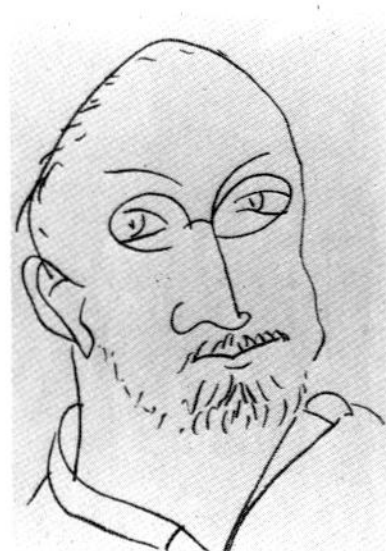

Ernest Pignon

"Matisse possesses the secret of revealing the world to us in images that have a freshness and intelligence of means that delight us.
"In his pictures form and colour blossom with happiness because they are used with a sense of economy and unity which he is perhaps alone in possessing to such an extent.
We are no longer talking about a fragment of nature, nor 'a window on life', but an organic whole in which the trembling of sensations perceived in nature is admirably conveyed by visual equivalents which amaze us.
"Most young people owe him their taste for vibrant colour and its organisation in a way that expresses, as well as a kinship to the fresco painters of Saint-Savin and Tavant, to which Matisse returned and which his recent canvases shown at the Autumn Salon strikingly confirm."
November 1948.

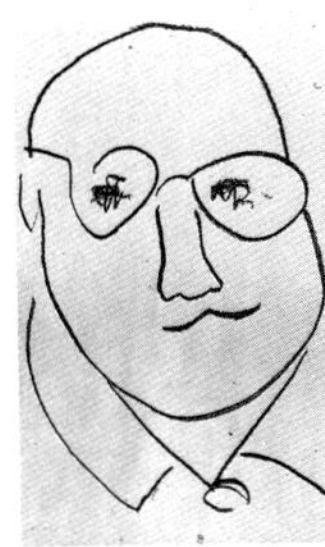

Georges Duthuit

"During Matisse's funeral the weather was cloudy and rather dull in Nice. But when, after the service, the cortège reformed to take his body to its last resting place high up in Cimiez, the sun's rays suddenly split the grey canvas and blooded the sky with exactly the same radiance, the same welcoming glow that Matisse had struggled to catch and reflect throughout his whole life.... Without being sentimental about it, it was hard not to think – simply because that was how it was – that the sun too had tried to pay a tribute of sympathy to his most faithful servant, and that his appearance at that time was telling us that he had come as a witness to bear witness to the light."
"Le tailleur de lumière", *Verve*, 1958.

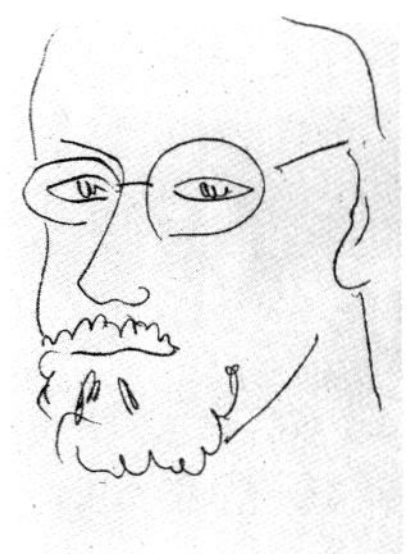

Jean Cassou

"In Matisse's last creations there is a kind of smile. The smile of the intellect that says, 'why not?' or again: 'is that all it is?' [...]
Greatness is the quality we recognise, supremely, in the work of Henri Matisse: work of light, admirable work, an honour to the French genius, an enchantment for future humanity."
Preface to the catalogue of the Henri Matisse retrospective exhibition, 1956, MNAM, Paris.

Glossary

Arabesque
From the Italian *arabesco*, meaning a line forming an ideal curve, which links the elements of a painted or sculpted composition.

Brush stroke
The way colour is applied.

Burin
Name of an engraving tool and the technique associated with its use. It allows for clear, strong lines, delicate nuances and varied tones.

Ceramic
From the Greek *keramon*, meaning "clay". Earthenware, china or porcelain pottery.

Charcoal
Burnt wood. Usually used for making preliminary sketches.

Chiaroscuro
The use of diffuse light on a dark background. Chiaroscuro brings out contrasts of dark and light.

Chromatic
From the Greek *chromos*, meaning "colour". Belonging to colour.

Collage
A technique involving assembling and sticking fragments of different materials, particularly pieces of cut paper, on to a background material.

Composition
The formal arrangement of the scene painted or drawn; the lines of composition structure the picture.

Complementary colours
Each primary colour has a corresponding secondary colour that heightens it; green is the complementary colour of red, violet of yellow and orange of blue.

Copy
Imitation or reproduction of a work of art; not to be confused with an "interpretation", which is the creation of an independent work, inspired by a work of art (practised notably by Picasso).

Dry point
Engraving technique in which a steel stylus is used directly on a copper plate, and the resulting "burr" is left in place. Also applied to the tool and the print made by this process.

Easel
A standing frame that supports a picture while it is being worked on.

Engraving
The art of creating shapes by cutting into any surface.
The name given to the result obtained by printing from the engraved and inked material, usually on to paper.
Depending on the process used, engraving can be done on wood (to produce a wood engraving or woodcut), metal (to produce a burin or an etching), stone (by lithography) or linoleum (to produce a linocut).

Etching
The process of engraving metal by using an acid. The word is used for both the technique and the print itself.

Fauvism

An artistic movement that appeared in 1905 and owes its name to a critic's jibe. For a few years it included some of the main painters of the 20th century (such as Matisse, Derain, Vlaminck, Van Dongen, Braque and Dufy).
This style of painting was characterised by heightened colour (bearing no relation to the colour of the object represented), a rejection of perspective, space, light and Impressionist naturalism.

Flat colour

Uniformly applied colour without brush marks or shading.

Gouache

Water-based paint, and the work so produced, in which pigment is bound with glue and made more opaque than watercolour by adding white. Colours can easily be superimposed.

Lithography

From the Greek *lithos*, meaning "stone", and *graphein*, "to write". The technique of producing prints of designs drawn directly on limestone with a greasy chalk. The stone is wetted, and greasy ink adheres to the chalk but not to the damp stone. Discovered in 1796 by Aloïs Senefelder.

Mythology

From the Greek *mythos*, meaning "fable", and *logos*, "knowledge". Mythology consists of fantastic stories about ancient gods and heroes.

Oil paint

Paint made of ground pigment bound with oil that dries easily, usually linseed. Oil paint can be used on any material that has been prepared with a coating in advance.

Paint layer

The layer on a canvas between the preparatory coating and the varnish. It usually includes the sketch, the first version, the intermediate layer of colour and the final version.

Palette

Word used for a round, oval or rectangular surface on which to mix paint; and also for the range of tones or colours used by a painter.

Pastel

Material made from a mixture of powdered colour and ground white gypsum, formed into a paste with glue or gum arabic. Comes most often in a crayon-like shape. The term also refers to the picture done with pastel crayons.

Pigment

Substance from which a colour is made. Pigment can be organic, inorganic or chemical in origin and must be mixed with a liquid before being used in painting.

Rough sketch

A preparatory drawing which gives the essential lines. A rough sketch precedes studies and sketches. It is done in pencil, pen or colour.

Primary colours

Red, yellow and blue. These colours provide the basic elements from which all other colours are derived.

Print

A printed image produced by being engraved or drawn on a material, usually metal, wood, stone or a lithographic plate.

Pure colours

Pure colours are applied without prior mixing straight from the tube or pot.

Relief
The imitation of three dimensions on a flat surface.

Secondary colours
Green, violet and orange. Each of these is made by mixing two primary colours.

Shade
The variety or degree of colour obtained by mixing several colours. The term also refers to various types of the same colour; for example a range of blues includes cobalt, indigo, Prussian Blue and ultramarine.

Sketch
First stage of a work, indicating the overall subject and the main parts. A sketch may be drawn with pen or pencil or painted on a canvas.

Stencil
Cardboard or metal cut to a particular shape, which is brushed with paint to create the design whose shape has been cut out. This technique is widely used to reproduce designs on material or wall-paper.

Stretcher
Wooden frame across which the canvas to be painted is stretched and then fixed.

Study
Drawing or painting that precedes the final picture. Usually the painter studies some elements of the composition in detail (such as anatomy, groups or draperies).

Support
The solid material on which the pictorial layer is laid. The most commonly used supports are canvas, paper and wood.

Surrealism
A literary and artistic movement whose aim was to free the psyche by mixing reason and unreason and moral and aesthetic considerations.

Thinning
A gradual lessening of a colour's brilliance. Thinning takes a colour through all the degrees of value.

Tone
The value or degree of intensity of a shade or colour, from darkest to lightest.

Underpainting layer
Coat of thinned colour applied uniformly before the painting proper is begun.

Value
The value of a tone means its degree of intensity in relation to light and shadow. It can also be described in terms of its degree of coldness or warmth.

Watercolour
Water-based coloured paint in which pigments are bound with gum arabic; more transparent than gouache. Applied to paper or card. The word is also used for the finished work.

Woodcut
Block of wood with a design, cut along the grain, from which prints are made. The word also applies to the print itself.

Wood engraving
The art of engraving designs on wood by cutting across the grain. The word also applies to the wood that has been cut in this way and the print taken from it.

Photographic credits

© ADAGP, Paris, 1992, 1999: pp. 32-3, 50, 80, 86, 86-7, 94, 95 right, 96, 97, 107.
Artephot, Paris: pp. 22 - photo Plassart, 34 bottom - photo Plassart, 72 - photo Jourdain, 75 - photo Plassart, 87 top - photo Plassart.
Bibliothèque Nationale, Paris: pp. 37, 58, 59, 61, 77, 83, 93, 96, 103, 109.
DR: pp. 10, 11, 13, 32, 33, 88 top, 90 top, 97.
Éditions Scala, Paris: pp. 29 bottom right, 36, 66 left, 85.
MNAM, Centre Georges Pompidou: pp. 9 - photo Schall, 14 top - photo Gliksman, 14 bottom, 15, 16 bottom left - photo Bahier, 16 top right, 16 bottom right, 18 top, 18 bottom - photo Migeat, 20 - photo Bahier and Migeat, 26, 27, 30, 41 top - photo Purcell, 41 bottom - photo Migeat, 42, 44, 46, 53, 60, 64 left, 64 right - photo Hyde, 66 top right, 66 bottom right - photo Hyde, 68 bottom right, 68 left, 74, 76 - photo Migeat, 80 - photo Migeat, 84 - photo H. Adant, 86 top, 86-7, 95 right, 98 - photo Hyde, 102, 105 - photo H. Adant, 113 top, 117.
Musée Matisse, Le Cateau-Cambrésis: pp. 12 top, 24, 48, 71.
Musée Matisse, Nice: pp. 12 bottom, 48 bottom, 50 - photo H. Adant, 51, 54, 95 top left - photo H. Adant, 104 - photo H. Adant, 115 bottom, 115 top - photo H. Adant, 116 - photo H. Adant.
Photothèque des musées de la ville de Paris by SPADEM 1992: p. 49.
Photos archives Matisse: pp. 21, 31, 55, 62-3, 64 right, 79, 90 bottom, 92, 110, 112, 113 bottom, 114.
Photos Flammarion, Paris: pp. 34 top left, 38 left, 40, 47, 52, 56-7, 59 top, 68 top right, 70, 74, 78 top, 82, 100.
Rapho, Paris: p. 88 bottom - photo I. Bandy.
RMN, Paris: pp. 23, 25, 28, 29 bottom left, 38 right, 39, 40, 50 bottom, 65, 73, 81, 94.
Scala Instituto Fotografico Editoriale, Florence: p. 106
Statens Museum for Kunst, Copenhagen: pp. 34 top right - photo Petersen, 78 bottom - photo Petersen.
Studio Cathédrale, Metz: p. 107.
© Succession Picasso 1999, Paris: p. 73.

Copy-editor: Moira Johnston
Cover: Thierry Renard
Graphic Design: Maxence Scherf
Layout and composition: Jérome Faucheux
Photoengraving (text): Daïchi, Singapore
Photoengraving (cover): Offset Publicité, Paris
Printed by Arti Gafiche E.Gajani, Rozzano - Milan
Copyright registered April 1999